T. A. Kantonen

A Theology for Christian Stewardship

Wipf and Stock Publishers
EUGENE, OREGON

Wipf and Stock Publishers
150 West Broadway
Eugene, Oregon 97401

A Theology for Christian Stewardship
By Kantonen, T.A.
Copyright©1956 Augsburg Fortress
ISBN: 1-57910-817-2
Publication Date: November, 2001
Previously published by Muhlenberg Press, 1956.

All Bible quotations, unless otherwise specified,
are from the Revised Standard Version.

A Theology for
Christian Stewardship

TO FRANCES

whose graciousness in sharing
life's stewardship with me has
not wavered even in those trying
seasons when I have been with book

Foreword

In recent years the word *stewardship*, long familiar to American churchgoers, has been introduced into the thought and speech of Christians everywhere, thanks to the pioneering efforts of world leaders of the stewardship movement, such as Dr. Clarence C. Stoughton and Dr. Arthur H. Limouze. Everyone who has had a part in seeking to acquaint Christians in other lands with American church life has had to face the question: What is this thing that you call stewardship? If it represents only clever means which practical-minded Americans have devised for raising money, interest in it soon subsides. But if it can be shown to be vital Christian faith in action, revealing its power to transform all areas of life, then it raises the hope that here may be the beginning of a new awakening and renewal, a new coming of the Spirit. The fulfilment of this hope, both in America and elsewhere, demands a greater depth in our approach to stewardship, an exploration of its full potentialities in the light of the theology of the Christian gospel.

The thoughts expressed in this book did not originate entirely in a theologian's study or lecture room. In the background are numerous occasions when the writer has been called upon to apply his theology to the practical work of stewardship either as parish pastor or as lecturer to stewardship conferences, both Lutheran and interdenominational, both at home and abroad. The direct incentive for putting this thinking into the form of a book came from the annual meeting of the Joint Department of Stewardship and Benevolence of the National Council of Churches held at Wittenberg College in December, 1954. The stewardship leaders who heard the three lectures which I delivered at this meeting on the theological foundations of stewardship expressed the wish that they be used as a nucleus for a needed book on this subject. In carrying out this wish I have been led to expand the study far beyond the scope of the original lectures until the result is a concise but comprehensive summary of all the major doctrines of evangelical theology viewed in the perspective of their bearing upon stewardship. In the large and growing literature on stewardship there is, to my knowledge, no previous work which attempts such a task. In working on this virgin soil I have learned to appreciate anew the inexhaustible vitality and the perennial timeliness of the eternal gospel, as well as the importance of the concept of stewardship as a key for understanding and applying the truth of the gospel.

My primary source has been the New Testament, and I trust that my constant references to it will not be construed as static proof texts but as evidences of the application of the dynamic view of the Word presented in Chapter II. And if I have leaned heavily on Luther in the interpretation of the living message of the gospel, it is not in the interest of denominationalism (Lutherans indeed have no monopoly on Luther!), but because I know no better guide to the heart of the gospel.

My special thanks are due to President Stoughton of Wittenberg College, inspiring leader who has blazed the trail here followed and without whose encouragement this book would not have been written.

It is my earnest hope that this book will serve the twofold purpose of affording ministers and theological students a bridge from doctrinal theology to the actual life and work of the church and helping Christian laymen to obtain a firmer grasp of the Christian truth which gives substance and purpose to their activities in the Lord's service.

Springfield, Ohio
Christmastide, 1955

T. A. KANTONEN

Table of Contents

CHAPTER I

Stewardship and Theology

A European professor of theology who had heard for the first time a lecture on the theology of stewardship remarked to the lecturer that the stewardship program of the church, if it is deeply rooted in living theology, may come to have the same significance for the twentieth century that the revival of world missions had for the nineteenth century. Bishop Hanns Lilje has recently made an even more striking statement: "To know that with all that we are and all that we have we are God's stewards is the answer to a particularly deep yearning of the time in which we live, namely, the yearning for a *vita nova*, a complete renewal of our life. Here the insights of our American brethren in the faith have, in the perspective of church history, something like the same significance as the lessons which the German Lutheran Reformation has taught us about justification by grace, or the Communion of the Brethren about the unity of God's children." [1]

A "theology for stewardship" may appear at first sight to be a strange combination of words. Theology is supposed to be the occupation of a small group of academic men who carry on their endless analyses and debates in ivory towers of spiritual learning, quite removed from the everyday interests of ordinary Christians. Stewardship, on the other hand, suggests such a mundane thing as money and is considered to be the concern of practical men of action who have little use for the subtleties of theology as they seek to devise methods for meeting budgets. Yet any serious attempt to define the two terms reveals at once an inseparable connection between them. Theology may be de-

---

[1] The foreword to *Als die guten Haushalter* by Heinrich Rendtorff (Neuendettelsau: Freimund-Verlag, 1952).

fined briefly in the words of Kahnis as "the scientific self-consciousness of the church" or of Luthardt as "the churchly science of Christianity." Althaus describes it as the consummation of the act of faith in the realm of thought. It is the church's effort to think through as fully and coherently as possible the meaning of its faith and life. Even if stewardship, then, dealt only with the Christian's use of his pocketbook, it would still be of theological concern, for theology cannot be indifferent to any activity in which the Christian faith expresses itself. But stewardship is more than that. It is the *vita nova*, the believer's whole life as a response to that revelation of divine truth with which theology deals. Theology thus has the same relation to stewardship that a philosophy of life has to life itself. And a theology of stewardship can be nothing less than an interpretation of the Christian meaning of life as a whole.

Stewardship is the English word used to translate the New Testament word *oikonomia*. The Greek word is a compound of *oikos*, meaning house, and *nomos*, meaning law. It refers thus to the management of a house or of household affairs. In classical Greek it had a variety of connotations but principally that of financial administration, the meaning retained in its direct derivatives such as economy and economics. In the Gospels an *oikonomos*, steward, is a slave or hired servant to whom the owner entrusts the management of his household. "Who then is the faithful and wise steward, whom his master will set over his household, to give them their portion of food at the proper time?" [2] The term acquires a spiritual significance, however, when our Lord uses it as a metaphor to describe a man's management of his whole life in responsibility to God. In the Pauline epistles *oikonomia* becomes a definite religious concept. Paul uses it in defining his commission as preacher of the gospel.[3] He

[2] Luke 12:42. Cf. Luke 16:1-9, Matt. 20:8.
[3] I Cor. 9:17.

2

speaks of himself as steward of the grace of God[4] and of the mysteries of God.[5] He even resorts to this term to define Christ's administration of God's redemptive plan for the world. Stewardship obtains its highest meaning and its strongest theological foundation when the apostle relates it to God's purpose "which he set forth in Christ as a plan [literally stewardship plan, *oikonomia*] for the fulness of time, to unite all things in him, things in heaven and things on earth." [6]

A term with such a wealth of meaning is difficult to translate. English translations of the Bible have had recourse to such supplementary words as dispensation, plan, and commission, to express its various shades of meaning. But when the old word stewardship takes on the new depth and richness which it has acquired in American church life, it is still the best single equivalent of the Pauline *oikonomia*. The word itself seems to have a still more humble origin than *oikonomia*. It first appears in Old English as *stiweard* or *stigweard*, formed from *sti* or *stig*, meaning hall, and *weard*, meaning warden or keeper. Since *sti* came to have the meaning which it still retains in *sty*, it would not be amiss to render the literal meaning of steward as sty warden, keeper of swine. Already in Middle English, however, it had general reference to anyone who manages the household or property of another. It was therefore the logical word to use for *oikonomos* in the early English translations of the New Testament. In modern usage it applies specifically to a ship's officer who has charge of the provisions and rooms of the passengers or to an employee of a club who manages the table and the servants. As in the case of the New Testament use of *oikonomia*, the literal and popular meaning of the word can serve only as a figure of speech for the religious idea it is used to convey.

It is not easy to express the religious meaning of stewardship in a language in which there has been no such sublimation of the

[4] Eph. 3:2. [5] I Cor. 4:1. [6] Eph. 1:9-10.

3

word used for it. The German word *Haushalterschaft*, for example, retains too faithfully the economic connotation of the *oikonomia* of classical Greek. Various substitutes have been offered ranging from *Treuhaenderschaft*, trusteeship, to *Liebesdankbarkeit*, gratitude of love. Each of them expresses some important aspect of stewardship but not its full significance. The disposition today is to give up the search for a new word and either to endow *Haushalterschaft* with a richer meaning or simply use the English word stewardship. I encountered the same difficulty in lecturing on stewardship to the clergy of Finland. *Taloudenhoito*, the standard Finnish word for *oikonomia*, refuses to take on more than a purely economic meaning, while *huoneenhallitus*, the word used in the newest translation, adheres still more literally to the sense of management of a household. In desperation I introduced a new word, *huoltovastuu*, compounded of *huolto*, care or trusteeship, and *vastuu*, responsibility. An adequate concept of stewardship must certainly contain both of these ingredients. As Dr. W. H. Greever has pointed out, trusteeship by itself refers to the passive reception of possessions while stewardship includes also the active and responsible administration of that which has been received as a trust.[7]

When the concept of stewardship is developed in its total New Testament context it implies even more than trusteeship and responsibility. It contains the idea of partnership. The relation between master and servant gives way to the relation between friends working together for the realization of a common purpose. Thus in speaking to his disciples about their stewardship responsibility of fruitful service our Lord says, "No longer do I call you servants, for the servant does not know what his master is doing; but I have called you friends, for all that I have heard from my Father I have made known to you." [8] And Paul

[7] *Workers with God* (Philadelphia: United Lutheran Publication House, 1921), pp. 23-25.   [8] John 15:15.

4

ascribes to Christian stewards the dignity of being God's fellow-workers.[9] This partnership is furthermore the partnership of father and son: "You are no longer a slave but a son, and if a son then an heir." [10] Christian stewardship is a family affair. Not merely to work for God as his agents and administrators of his property, but to work with him as his children, sharing his purposes, his resources, his very nature—such is the high status of Christian stewards.

The interest in stewardship in the American churches has had, for the most part, an intensely practical motivation. Ours is a land in which church membership is altogether a matter of personal commitment. The church receives no financial support whatever from the state. Both the local congregations and the organized church at large with all its manifold structures and activities rest entirely upon the voluntary giving of church members. Under these conditions it is just as easy to understand why the American churches have sought to stimulate liberal and regular contribution of funds as it is to explain why the tax-supported churches of Europe have been correspondingly lax in this matter. While our European brethren have been in position to develop what they often regard as a more "spiritual" type of religion, we have been led to relate our faith to the material realities of life and to look upon the giving of money as the "acid test" of the genuineness of a man's commitment to Christ.

It is to the credit of the early leaders of the stewardship movement that even when their primary interest was the raising of large sums of money they condemned unequivocally all unscriptural and unchristian methods for achieving this end. Hence along with the steady increase of freewill offerings we have witnessed the gradual disappearance of sales and suppers, bazaars and lotteries. But in combing the Scriptures for the passages that could be used to accelerate giving we have also been tempted to

[9] I Cor. 3:9.   [10] Gal. 4:7.

follow shortcuts leading away from the main highway of Christian truth. The greatest danger has been to compromise the gospel through moralism and legalism drawn from the Old Testament. Thus the tithe has assumed a far greater prominence than it has in the New Testament and has often been advocated on grounds quite different from the spirit of the gospel. And our stewardship literature abounds in promises of prosperity to those who fulfil their obligations to God. Too often the stewardship appeal rests on impersonal laws and principles and its target is the enlightened self-interest of unregenerate human nature. Less evident is the joyful gratitude of the Christian man to whom stewardship is the expression of his personal fellowship with his Lord.

It is high time therefore to examine stewardship from the point of view of the theology of the gospel. A clear view of the intimate relation between evangelical theology and stewardship is of vital concern to both. Both have their starting point in an encounter with the living Christ. Theology seeks to think out the meaning of that encounter. Stewardship seeks to live it out. A theology that fails to relate itself to the vital issues of Christian activity shrivels into lifeless intellectualism, a sterile preoccupation with abstract concepts. And a stewardship that is not rooted in clear and sound theological convictions degenerates into shallow activism and loses its distinctive Christian character.

Thoughtful leaders of the stewardship movement have not been blind to the necessity of finding a theological basis for their work. The earliest attempts to meet this need suffered, however, from an orientation to the romantic moralism of the old "social gospel." Thus John M. Versteeg's exploration of *The Deeper Meaning of Stewardship* led him to regard stewardship as "the word of the social gospel made flesh." [11] The current resurgence of evangelical theology has brought greater depth. One of the outstanding pioneers in the application of this approach is W. H.

[11] New York: Abingdon Press, 1923, p. 9.

Greever. The clarity and breadth of his outlook are revealed in his oft-quoted words, "Christian stewardship is the *practice* of the Christian religion. It is neither a department of life nor a sphere of activity. It is the Christian conception of life as a whole, manifested in attitudes and actions." [12] The theology undergirding this position is summed up in another terse statement: "The motive for all Christian service is love and gratitude; the purpose is to glorify God, through the salvation of souls; the guide is the revealed will of God; the measure is ability, in the sacrificial spirit of Christ; the efficiency is the power of God's grace, working through obedient human agency; the reward is a good conscience and the anticipated 'well done' of the Lord." [13] The life of stewardship is nothing less than "total devotion" to the Christ who is known as a "real, living personal presence in the hearts of believers," a genuine loyalty that is expressed not in mere opinion or sentiment but in character and conduct.

The evangelical approach has obtained a world-wide hearing through an ecumenical leader of the stewardship movement, Clarence C. Stoughton, whose constant emphasis is on the response which the believer makes with his whole life to God's redeeming grace. Stewardship to him is "human thanksgiving for divine goodness and mercy." [14] The grace note is clearly sounded also in Amos J. Traver's *Gracious Giving*, nor is it missing in such special studies as Holmes Rolston's discriminating analysis of *Stewardship in the New Testament Church* and Bishop V. S. Azariah's *Christian Giving*. Particularly promising are the pioneering studies, deeply grounded in the New Testament, made recently in Germany by Heinrich Rendtorff, Herbert Reich, and Wilhelm Thomas. The most comprehensive systematic presentation of the theology of stewardship on the basis of the gospel

[12] W. H. Greever, *Work of the Lord* (New York: Revell, 1937), p. 62.
[13] W. H. Greever, *Realities in the Christian Religion*, private printing, 1951, p. 109.
[14] *Whatever You Do* (Philadelphia: Muhlenberg Press, 1949), p. 28.

7

is a doctoral dissertation by A. C. Conrad entitled *The Divine Economy*. The author defines stewardship as "partnership with Christ, through the Holy Spirit, in fulfilling the purpose of God in the world." [15] His analysis of the divine purpose is penetrating and well founded. He is chiefly concerned, however, with applying the concept of stewardship to God's own activity rather than to the believer's response. Only a single chapter is devoted to "the stewardship of the believer."

In conceiving of stewardship as the response of faith we acknowledge indeed that God has revealed to us his plan for ordering all of life and that the initiative in carrying it out belongs to him. We speak about him only because he has first spoken to us. We love because he first loved us. We give because he first gave. Our religion is not a struggle to develop our own spiritual resources in order to rise to his level. It is a joyful acceptance of the divine resources to which we have access because he has descended to our level. Since this way of God to man, which supplants man's futile attempt to reach God, is Christ, the theology of the gospel is radically Christ-centered theology. In him God not only speaks to us but comes to us. He is God incarnate, God in saving action, God reaching out for us. In him God not only reveals to us his mind and will but receives us into his fellowship. Our commitment is not to any impersonal policy or doctrine, any set of principles or regulations. It is personal loyalty to him who loved us and gave himself for us. The keynote of this Christ-centered theology is grace. Its motivation for action has the quality of overflowing spontaneity which excludes all legalistic coercion and striving for merit. We do not have to bargain with God: if I do this for you, will you do that for me? We do not have to buy his favor. It is he who has already bought us with a price. We do not need to work slavishly

[15] A. C. Conrad, *The Divine Economy* (Grand Rapids: Eerdmans, 1955), p. 27.

to win his friendship. He has already given us the status of sons. If the aim of stewardship were only to achieve practical results, such as the securing of money for a worthy cause, any kind of theology serving this purpose would be justified. Recently a prominent member of the Roman Catholic hierarchy addressed a group of workers in a community chest campaign thus: "The contributions which you make and secure will be recorded in your book of life. They will constitute your treasure in heaven." This is an echo of the popular couplet used in connection with Tetzel's sale of indulgences, which precipitated the Reformation:

> "Soon as the groschen in the casket rings,
> The soul from purgatory springs."

Here is a type of theology which has lost none of its effectiveness for the purpose of raising money. It is the theology of Protestants too when they present their offerings to God in the expectation of receiving blessings in return. But it is not the theology of the gospel and it has nothing to do with the stewardship based upon the gospel. The treasure of our stewardship is the riches of God's grace freely bestowed upon us in Christ and appropriated by faith as capital for a new life in partnership with God.

In an earlier study I have presented stewardship as the living expression of the total content of the Christian faith and outlined its theology in terms of the threefold Christian creed, faith in God the Father, the Son, and the Holy Spirit. The conclusions reached were summarized as follows: "From the doctrine of creation we derive the concepts of God's sovereignty and our trusteeship and responsibility. From the doctrine of redemption we derive our insight into the grace which restores sinners into fellowship with God and awakens the gratitude, joy, and love which motivate us to give our lives to our Redeemer. From the doctrine of sanctification we derive our understanding of the living faith which, drawing upon God's resources, bears fruit in obedience and dedicated service. Faith in God the Creator establishes evangelism and stewardship as God's work. Faith in God the Redeemer establishes the basis on which sinful men can do God's work. Faith in God the Sanctifier consecrates us to the doing of this work." [16]

This outline needs now to be filled and expanded. There are questions of fundamental importance to the theology of the gospel which demand a more specific answer. What is the nature of the Word which since the days of the Reformation has been accepted as the vehicle of divine revelation and the norm of all faith and life? What is the Christian view of God, of the world, and of man, which underlies the conception of life as stewardship? How is stewardship related to the centrality and the sovereignty of Christ? What is the meaning of that pivotal encounter with God which Paul and the Reformers described as justification by grace? What are the stewardship implications of the doctrine that all believers are priests? What does it mean to stewardship to conceive the church as the creation of the Holy Spirit and the body of Christ? What role does the hope of reward play in the life of stewardship? It is by answering such questions that theology can use its insights into the gospel to vitalize and guide the practice of the Christian religion.

[16] *The Lutheran Quarterly*, August, 1951, p. 277.

CHAPTER II

Stewardship and the Word of God

God spoke, and the world came into being. God continues to speak, and his purposes in the world are accomplished. This is the keynote of both the Old Testament and the New. "For as the rain and the snow come down from heaven, and return not thither but water the earth, making it bring forth and sprout, giving seed to the sower and bread to the eater, so shall my word be that goes forth from my mouth; it shall not return to me empty, but it shall accomplish that which I purpose, and prosper in the thing for which I sent it." [1] "For the word of God is living and active, sharper than any two-edged sword." [2] The Word is God himself in creative action, and any activity that purports to represent the will of God must be founded upon the Word of God.

This is also the keynote of evangelical theology. The Reformation was not hatched in a vacuum. It grew out of fresh deep insight into God's Word. Hence the Word, and no human authority, came to be the foundation of the church, the judge and guide of every aspect of its faith and work. In Luther's magnificent expresssion, "Tota vita et substantia ecclesiae est in verbo Dei," the whole life and substance of the church is in the Word of God. The discovery of God's Word meant freedom from the conflicting and misleading opinions of men. It meant: God has spoken. A sovereign and decisive word has been spoken concerning the whole business of living. The master plan of the structure of life, drawn by the Maker himself, has been revealed. More than that, God still speaks. His living Word provides both the guidance and the resources for the realization of his plan.

[1] Isa. 55:10-11.   [2] Heb. 4:12.

Here is a matter of pivotal importance to stewardship. By what right do we ask people to invest their time and energy and property, their very selves, in the church? Do we offer surmises and theories as to why this is a sound investment? Do we appeal to their generosity and their self-interest? Or can "Thus saith the Lord" be attached to what we are saying and doing? If God has not spoken, we are merely manipulating human motives toward human goals. If God has spoken, our chief concern is not how to perfect our techniques and whip up our enthusiasms but how to be obedient to what he has to say. Paul stated the basic method of Christian stewardship, and of all Christian work, when he said, "We refuse to practice cunning or to tamper with God's word, but by the open statement of the truth we would commend ourselves to every man's conscience in the sight of God." [3] It makes a vast difference in the nature of the stewardship appeal whether it is one man drawing upon his ingenuity and resourcefulness to interest another man in a good cause, or whether it is God himself who lays claim to a man's whole life, saying, "I am the Lord thy God; thou shalt have no other gods [such as mammon] before me."

If stewardship, then, is to be founded upon the Word of God, it is necessary to have a clear understanding of the nature and function of the Word. What do we mean when we say "the Word of God"? It will not do simply to identify the Word with Scripture. According to Scripture itself, the title "the Word of God" belongs primarily to Christ. He is God's self-revelation to men. "The Word was God . . . the Word became flesh and dwelt among us." [4] "The name by which he is called is The Word of God." [5] He is "the Alpha and the Omega," the alphabet of God's communication to us, "the first and the last" mediator of God's life to us, "the beginning and the end" of what God means to us. In the Christian message it is not an institution or

[3] II Cor. 4:2.   [4] John 1:1, 14.   [5] Rev. 19:13.

12

a book or a body of doctrine that asks for our trust and allegiance but a person who says, "I am the truth" and "He who has seen me has seen the Father."

The Word of God in its derivative sense is the life-changing message of God's redeeming activity in Christ, the gospel. We may describe it as a centrifugal "power of God unto salvation" proceeding from the midpoint of revelation, Christ, and reaching forth to the ends of the earth and to the close of history. For the apostles, to whom the gospel was first committed, its content was the crucified and risen Christ and his constant power to make God a living reality to men. To preach the Word was to preach Christ. But the apostles were convinced that where Christ was preached there Christ himself was present, making good his promise, "I am with you always." Hence "they went forth and preached everywhere, while the Lord worked with them and confirmed the message." [6] It is Christ's own presence that makes the gospel truly a "means of grace." The gospel does more than tell "the old, old story of Jesus and his love." It is the means by which Jesus himself confronts men. It does not point beyond itself to something high and holy toward which we are to strive. It brings God in his holiness and love to us. It is God's Word not because it speaks about God but because in it God speaks. Just as in the creation of the world God spoke and the world began, so today God speaks in the word of the gospel and new life is created in human hearts. That is the way Paul conceived the message which he proclaimed: "It is the God who said, 'Let light shine out of darkness,' who shone in our hearts to give the light of the knowledge of the glory of God in the face of Christ." [7] That is why he could say, "My speech and my message were not in plausible words of wisdom, but in demonstration of the Spirit and power." [8]

The original way in which the gospel was communicated was

[6] Mark 16:20. [7] II Cor. 4:6. [8] I Cor. 2:4.

by word of mouth. Christ himself wrote nothing, neither did most of the apostles. The spoken proclamation of the Word preceded its written form. Whether through public preaching or through informal "gossiping the gospel" in personal contacts, the voice was the principal medium by which the church of the apostles and martyrs spread the good news. Christians bore witness to the Word and died for the Word without the benefit of a written New Testament. The church simply adopted the Bible of the Jews and gave it a new interpretation. It saw in Christ the fulfilment of the Old Testament law, prophecy, and sacrifice. Thus the Hebrew Bible became transformed into a Christ-book. When the Jew reads his Bible, says Paul, its true vital content, the message of redemption, remains veiled. Only in Christ is the veil removed.

As time went on, it became necessary to put the apostolic message itself in writing. When the apostle Paul, the first of the New Testament writers, found it necessary to write letters explaining the Christian faith and life to the congregations he had founded, his writing had the same source, the same content, and the same inspiration as his preaching. And as the events in the early life of our Lord faded farther and farther into history, other apostles and their associates were led by the same Spirit who inspired all their work to draw up brief written accounts of his life and teaching. Thus the apostolic witness obtained the enduring form of the New Testament. That the purpose of the written form of the Word was precisely the same as that of the original oral form is evident from the words of the author of the Fourth Gospel, "These [things] are written that you may believe that Jesus is the Christ, the Son of God, and that believing you may have life in his name." [9] Through the written Word the church retains an unbroken and uncorrupted continuity with the original Christian witness and provides for men in every age

[9] John 20:31.

an encounter with the Word that became flesh for us.

"The Bible," declared Archbishop Lehtonen of Finland, "differs from the sacred books of all other religions. They all speak of God who demands and man who acts, while the Bible speaks of God who acts and man who benefits from God's action." The uniqueness of the Bible lies in the uniqueness of Christ, and the authority of the Bible is the authority of Christ. The written Word, like the oral proclamation of the first Christians, bears witness to his saving sovereignty. Its central theme is the same as that of Peter on Pentecost, "God has made him both Lord and Christ, this Jesus whom you crucified." [10] It is the astounding good news that in the battle against sin and death victory belongs to the Crucified. A new age has begun. The whole context of human living has been changed. Christ is the head of a new race of redeemed men. He has dethroned the principalities and powers of evil and assumed lordship over all history. The power by which he overcame death is available to us as we await the inevitable consummation of his victory. The Word is an invitation to a personal encounter with the living Christ, an invitation to share the reality of his triumph. Christ's conquest of sin and death is of vital personal concern to every man, for "all have sinned and fall short of the glory of God," [11] and all have to face death. The Word is an announcement of the deliverance that has been won and a call to become participators in it. Why, asks Luther, should we fear the conquered power as though it were the conqueror? The Word finds its mark as it leads one man after another to say, "I have met my rightful Lord and risen with him into a newness of life. Here is one more in whom Christ's redeeming work has achieved its purpose, one more witness of the good news, one more Christian steward."

It is thus in the life of stewardship that the Word achieves its end and manifests its true dynamic character. The Word is not

[10] Acts 2:36.   [11] Rom. 3:23.

a collection of ideas to be understood or a set of rules to be obeyed but the power of a new life to be received. Its primary appeal is neither to the intellect nor the emotions but to the will and conscience, to man as man. It seeks to take hold of the total personality and to give not mere information about God but fellowship with God. It is not a general "to whom it may concern" but addresses itself, to use a good Quaker expression, "to our condition." It meets, not men's idle curiosity, but their anxiety, guilt, despair. It confronts men at the point of their deepest need. It both discloses and meets our need for a Savior. It brings to us not only new insight and wisdom on matters which constitute our ultimate concern but an entirely new structure of life, the rule of God, the sovereignty of Christ. It not only acquaints us with the sacred Scriptures but transforms us into living epistles of Christ. It not only makes known the reconciliation effected by Christ but commissions us to a ministry of reconciliation.

The nature of the Word as divine power operating through a human agency is in itself a profound example of stewardship. Paul applies to himself the term "steward of grace" when he realizes that as servant of the Word he is a man through whom Christ carries on his saving work. He uses a revealing metaphor to illustrate this stewardship: "we have this treasure in earthen vessels." [12] The context makes clear what the apostle means by "this treasure." God, he declares, has qualified us to be ministers of a new covenant, far more vital, radiant, and permanent than the covenant mediated by Moses. Its basis and substance is no written code but the dynamic gospel of the glory of Christ. This gospel carries saving power because it issues from the living Lord himself. The Word of God entrusted to the ministry of the new covenant is not our thoughts about God, not even God's thoughts handed down to us in transcript, but the very Word

[12] II Cor. 4:7.

that became flesh. "What we preach," says Paul, "is Jesus Christ," [13] and to prevent us from losing the force of that remarkable statement and twisting it to mean that we only talk about Christ the apostle goes on to say that we carry in our very bodies the crucified and risen Lord "that the life of Jesus may be manifested in our mortal flesh." [14] When we bear witness to our Lord, the miracle of the incarnation is duplicated and Jesus once more lives and speaks. Through us the kingdom of God touches the lives of other men, and God becomes real to them. So tremendous is the impact that it has the force of a new creation, as in the beginning when God made an ordered cosmos out of chaos. The Word entrusted to us is as creative as the Word by which the heavens were made. It shines into the chaos of ignorance, sin, and death with the power to recreate the disordered lives of men and to present them to God as new creatures in Christ.

This treasure we have when we have the gospel. But we have it in earthen vessels, says the apostle, referring to the frailty of that mortal flesh through which God has chosen to transmit the riches of his grace. His description of the earthen vessel is this: "We are afflicted in every way; . . . we are perplexed, . . . persecuted, . . . struck down, . . . death is at work in us." [15] It is not because of our own strength, but only because of the transcendent power of the treasure which we carry, that we are not crushed by our afflictions, driven to despair by our perplexities, destroyed by the blows we receive. No one who has read Sholem Asch's *The Apostle* is likely to forget his portrayal of the dreadful personal handicaps under which Paul carried on his ministry. It is doubtless overdramatization to picture the apostle as having only one eye and as being subject to epileptic seizures, but it is obvious at any rate that Paul's strength did not lie in his natural equipment or attractiveness. There was an inner resilience and toughness

[13] II Cor. 4:5.　　[14] II Cor. 4:11.　　[15] II Cor. 4:8-12.

17

about this externally frail man which enabled him not merely to triumph over his handicaps but to transform every thorn in the flesh into a handle for obtaining a firmer grip on God's grace.

The subsequent history of the church is replete with similar instances of the power of God made manifest through fragile earthen vessels. They all point to the method which God consistently uses in revealing himself. When he chooses a nation to be the carrier of his revelation, he passes by the glory and might of Egypt and Babylon, of Greece and Rome, and selects the despised little nation of Israel. And when he sends into the world his only begotten Son, the brightness of his glory and the express image of his person, he allows him to assume the form of a servant who has "no beauty that we should desire him." Blessed indeed is the one who is not offended at this lowly man who speaks with the authority of God. The supreme disclosure of God's sovereign love is through the shame of the cross. When the messianic nation, the church, is formed to be the body of Christ on earth, "not many wise, not many mighty, not many noble" are called, but God chooses "what is foolish . . . what is weak . . . what is low and despised in the world." [16] Again the form of a servant, the occasion for offense. The same applies to those transcripts of lost documents by which the faith once delivered to the saints has come down to us, the Scriptures. St. Chrysostom describes them as "all human as well as all divine." Those who concentrate their attention on the human side of the Bible, whether to criticize those aspects in which the scriptural writers were children of their day, or to idolize the scriptural text itself, deal only with the earthen vessel instead of the divine treasure. The same distinction holds finally also in the case of the visible Word, the sacraments, in which through unpretentious earthly elements the Lord communicates his saving presence. It is this Lord, whose glory is to use the most unlikely material as his instruments and

[16] I Cor. 1:26-28.

to make his strength perfect in weakness, who entrusts to us, earthen as we are, the treasure of our stewardship.

One other aspect of the Word, of unique importance to stewardship, needs to be pointed out; namely, the inseparable connection between the Word of God and the people of God, the Christian message and the Christian fellowship. Christianity in its essence is not an ideology or a code but a fellowship. The gospel establishes not only contemporaneity with Christ but unity with him, and this unity is not one of mere ideas but concrete unity with the body of Christ, the church. Apart from his body, Christ is not the Christ of the Christian faith. He may be known as teacher, prophet, or martyr, but not as Savior. The church is the new humanity of which he is the Head and into which we are incorporated when we accept the gospel. In the fellowship of his people he is experienced as a living presence. Outside the church, insists Bulgakoff, the Bible itself is an ordinary book which "dies in dead hands and becomes a mere object of criticism." It is in the church that it becomes the Word of God, the gospel of Christ, an instrument of his redemptive strategy, a means of grace. Christian truth has its vitality only as the functioning of the living body of Christ, and Christian living depends on the resources of the Christian fellowship. It is obvious, therefore, that our main task is not the teaching of Christian ideas or the promotion of Christian ideals. It is uniting men and women with the Christian church, extending and strengthening Christ-centered fellowship. Stewardship is consecration to this task.

In applying the evangelical concept of the Word to stewardship, particular attention must be given to a view which is diametrically opposed to it but which is widely prevalent in current stewardship literature. I refer to legalism, the use of the Bible as though it were a book of law containing regulations to be literally observed always and everywhere. From the point of view of the gospel the law belongs to a preparatory phase of divine revelation. "The law was our custodian until Christ came." [17] With Jesus the whole attempt to win God's favor by doing this or not doing that loses its validity. He provides such a revolutionary new insight into the holiness and love of God that it defies any codification. "It is as if in every one of his strenuous teachings Jesus were uttering the challenge, 'Try to make a law out of this if you can.' " [18] In place of external rules and regulations he sets up the personal relationship of love of God and of fellow-man, a relationship created and energized by God's own love. From this source Paul draws the foundation principles of Christian ethics: Christ is the end of the law for the Christian believer; love is the fulfilment of the law; Christian conduct is faith working through love. "Everything is permitted which Christian love permits" and "everything is demanded which Christian love requires." [19] The law, which in itself can never compel love to come into being or supply enabling power, can only reveal the lack of a right relation to God. Its function is perverted when it is used as a ladder to heaven or as a shackle upon Christian conscience.

As a specific case in point let us consider the law of *tithing*,[20] which has often been considered to be of fundamental importance in the scriptural teaching on Christian stewardship. The practice of paying tithes can be traced to hoary antiquity, at least as far back as the days of Abraham and Melchizedek,[21] but it has lost none of its usefulness as a practical aid to regularity in giving. As such it deserves to be encouraged. And it is just plain common sense, requiring no help from theology, to point out that the church would multiply its income and thus be enabled to make a vast expansion of its operations, if all its members were to contribute 10 per cent of their earnings to the work of the church.

---

[17] Gal. 3:24.
[18] Paul Ramsey, *Basic Christian Ethics* (New York: Scribner, 1950), p. 73.
[19] *Ibid.*, p. 79.
[20] Lev. 27:30-32.   [21] Gen. 14:20.

But tithing assumes theological significance when the motives underlying the practice are examined. When people ask how much they should give, the theology of the gospel does not permit us to reply simply, "The Word of God has the answer. You must give a tenth of your income. You must tithe, for God has commanded it." There are churches which regard the Old Testament law as having the same authority as the gospel and therefore impose the tithe as a condition of membership. The church of the New Testament cannot do this, for it has no right to attach primary importance to anything that is not included in the commission entrusted to it by its Lord, "teaching them to observe all that I have commanded you." The Lord gave no command concerning the tithe. Save for two incidental remarks, themselves critical in nature, which we shall examine presently, he made no reference to the tithe, and the gospel which he proclaimed transcends the entire legalistic dealing with God upon which the practice rested. Paul, the great theologian of the New Testament, never mentions it at all. From the point of view of his theology, it belongs with other Old Testament regulations to the law from which Christ has set us free.

But the tithe is not a unique or distinctive trait even of Old Testament religion. The Hebrews shared the practice with other ancient nations, such as the Greeks and the Romans, as well as with various primitive groups. It served to remind Israel of her covenant obligations to Yahweh, but unfortunately it also carried with it the connotation it has always had in natural religion, namely, that it is a means of obtaining divine favor, that in giving to God his stipulated due one has the right to expect something from him in return. This idea persists in the unknown minor prophet known as Malachi, "The Messenger," who portrays the withholding of tithes as "robbing God" and declares: "Bring the full tithes into the storehouse, that there may be food in my house; and thereby put me to the test, says the Lord of hosts, if

21

I will not open the windows of heaven for you and pour down for you an overflowing blessing." [22] The blessing is described in terms of the "fruits of your soil and your vine in the field." This sub-Christian text has often been used in appeals for Christian stewardship, although it is as incompatible with the spirit of the gospel as the curse which a vengeful psalmist pronounces on the babies of Babylon.[23] The inference that tithing guarantees material prosperity can be supported by numerous examples so long as one avoids negative instances of the prosperity of the wicked and the poverty and misfortune besetting many a tither. Already the great prophets of the Old Testament denounced strongly the expectation of inevitable earthly good fortune as a return from offerings made to God. Amos, Hosea, Micah, and Isaiah all declare repeatedly that God will not accept offerings or sacrifices prompted by motives unacceptable to him. In the only other specific prophetic reference to the tithe besides the one mentioned, Amos mocks the vain attempts of a sinful people to avert God's judgment by worship and tithing: "Come to Bethel, and transgress; to Gilgal, and multiply transgression; bring your sacrifices every morning, your tithes every three days." [24] Here the idea of putting God to a test assumes an entirely different meaning: go more often to your places of decadent worship and increase the frequency of your tithes and see if you can buy God's favor! So far from being influenced by their offerings, the prophet points out, God's providential care over his people was most clearly manifest at a time when they were unable to make him any offerings at all, during the forty years in the wilderness.[25]

Our Lord's two references to the tithe are in the same prophetic spirit. The first is: "Woe to you, scribes and Pharisees, hypocrites! for you tithe mint and dill and cummin, and have neglected the weightier matters of the law, justice and mercy and faith." [26] He does not condemn tithing as such, for he goes on

[22] Mal. 3:10.   [23] Ps. 137:9.   [24] Amos 4:4.   [25] Amos 5:25.
[26] Matt. 23:23; Luke 11:42.

to say, "These you ought to have done, without neglecting the others," but he stresses the relative unimportance of the punctilious tithing of the Pharisees in comparison with the "weightier matters." He describes the misplaced emphasis as "straining out a gnat and swallowing a camel." The other reference occurs in the parable of the Pharisee and the tax collector. The Pharisee's self-righteous prayer contains the boast, "I fast twice a week, I give tithes of all that I get." [27] Yet it is the tax collector, whose only offerings are a broken spirit and a contrite heart, who goes "down to his house justified rather than the other." It is worth adding that in another story involving a tax collector and "the weightier matters, justice and mercy and faith" the justified sinner who has received divine favor as a totally undeserved gift responds with spontaneous gratitude: "The half of my goods I give to the poor; and if I have defrauded any one of anything, I restore it fourfold." [28] Here is a freewill offering far above the tithe, flowing out of a righteousness that exceeds that of the scribes and the Pharisees.

In the light of this teaching of the prophets and of the Lord himself we see the superficiality of the view that tithing is the one divinely authorized and unconditionally binding method for practicing Christian stewardship. Not only does it lack a New Testament foundation but it lends itself to a man-centered legalism which imperils true religion. Not the least of the perils is the implication that having given God his 10 per cent I have discharged the full obligation of my stewardship and the remaining 90 per cent belongs to me to do with as I please. This is a flat contradiction of the basic Christian affirmation of the lordship of Christ over all of life. But when these perils are clearly recognized and the motives and objectives of tithing are supplied by the gospel, it is a practice to be commended and encouraged. There is as little reason to abandon it as there would be to discard

[27] Luke 18:12.   [28] Luke 19:8.

the practice of setting aside one day out of seven as the Lord's day simply because Christians are not bound by the sabbath regulations of the Old Testament. The practice of tithing, like habitual going to church on Sunday, may indeed serve the central purpose of the law, of being "custodian until Christ comes," preparing the way and providing the opportunity for a whole-hearted commitment to Christ. From the point of view of the gospel, the very question, "How much should I give?" indicates a spiritual immaturity marked by legalistic calculation instead of the overflowing spontaneity of the faith that works through love. It is the same type of question as Peter's question, "How often should I forgive my brother?" On that level tithing is as reasonable an answer to the question of giving as Peter's suggestion of seven is to the question of forgiving. The Lord's answer to Peter's question, "Not seven, but seventy times seven," indicates that his answer as to how much to give would be, "Not one-tenth, but ten times one-tenth."

The tithe, forgiveness, and the observance of the Lord's day come into their right Christian use when they are freely and joyfully practiced by Christians who do not give their Lord only one dollar out of ten or one day out of seven but whose whole life is stewardship. I am convinced that the tithers in our churches are by and large not Pharisees but humble and sincere Christians who have been led to use this ancient device as a helpful means for a steady expression of their gratitude and faithfulness to their Lord. In our secularized age, is it not in itself a sign of faith that a man dares, even to that extent, to loosen his grip on the almighty dollar in which worldly men put all their trust? But I am also convinced that the true beginning of Christian stewardship is in a clean break with the false god mammon through complete self-surrender to the love of God in Christ. The joyfully exuberant giving of the Macedonian Christians who out of extreme poverty gave, not according to their means, but beyond their means, earnestly begging for the privilege to give, was not the result of indoctrination in a coercive legal principle nor even stress on "proportionate giving." They gave because "first they gave themselves to the Lord." [29]

Not only in the matter of the tithe but in the presentation of stewardship in general the distinctive emphasis of evangelical Christianity is often conspicuously absent. The logic of the appeal proceeds as follows. God is the owner of everything. He has entrusted his property to us to be used according to his purpose. We must answer for that use before his judgment seat. We must therefore act as responsible and faithful stewards. This is sound logic as far as it goes, but it does not carry us one step beyond the Old Testament or even the Koran. There is not a trace in it of the gospel which as "the power of God unto salvation" transforms our status from that of steward in the original sense of hired servant to that of God's children. As stewards in the New Testament connotation we are "stewards of the manifold grace of God." The living center of our stewardship is Christ himself. It is a matter of our personal relationship to him, not the management of impersonal things according to impersonal codes and principles. We give ourselves as "a living sacrifice, holy and acceptable to God," [30] to him who loved us and gave himself for us. "We love, because he first loved us." [31] But we do "not love in word or speech but in deed and in truth." [32]

We have sought to analyze the meaning of the Word upon which our stewardship is based. But we have also discovered that this Christ-centered message of the new life calls for more than analysis. It invites both its proclaimers and its hearers to the venture of faith. It asks us to entrust ourselves wholeheartedly to that Christ who is the living Word. Perhaps I can make this plainer by means of an analogy from life. A half-century ago a

[29] II Cor. 8:1-5.   [30] Rom. 12:1.   [31] I John 4:19.   [32] I John 3:18.

25

man left his home in Europe, took his wife, his four-year-old son and his three daughters, and boarded an ocean liner bound for a new land, a land of freedom and opportunity. He had heard the message of the richer, fuller, freer life in the new land, and he had come to a decision to do something about it, although many ties were holding him back. As he walked the gangplank from the shore to the ship, he knew: I have left my former life behind; I have entrusted my future to this ship; I trust that it will carry me and my loved ones through night and storm to a more abundant life. And the children, sharing their parents' faith, sailed forth in the great adventure. This is a simple illustration and it has been duplicated in thousands of lives. This particular case comes close to me, for I was the four-year-old boy in the drama and it was my destiny too that was being decided. But does it not throw light on the Word of God and the response of stewardship? The Word is Christ's call to life eternal. We respond by entrusting ourselves to him. Our faith means that we dare to cross the gangplank from unbelief to belief, from trusting our own resources to entrusting ourselves to his grace. Hence we no longer live alone, but Christ lives in us. We are carried and supported. His saving and sustaining power in his Word and his church is like a ship that sails through the ocean of the world. We cast our burdens upon him. We discover again and again that our trust in him is not a trust misplaced. His Word is sure, his love the one constant among life's variables. And "having received this mercy we faint not," we do not lose heart or nerve in carrying out the responsibilities of the stewardship of this faith.

CHAPTER III

Stewardship and the Nature of God

"Thy nature, gracious Lord, impart," prays Charles Wesley in one of his finest hymns, concluding with "Write Thy new name upon my heart, Thy new, best name of love."

The nature of Christian stewardship, like all Christian thought and action, is derived from the Christian revelation of the nature of God. "God" in the sense of the ultimate principle of existence and the highest standard of value is of course no Christian monopoly. A Melanesian savage awed by *mana*, the wonder-working power which makes some objects *tabu*, and a French sociologist so obsessed with society that he regards God as only an idealized symbol of it, a poet who sees God in the structure of a flower in the crannied wall and another poet to whom God is another name for evolution, a philosopher whose God is synonymous with the universe and another philosopher whose God is only the value aspect of the universe—they all have a God of some sort. Atheism is not a formidable rival of Christianity but idolatry is. As Luther observed, everyone worships either *Gott* or *Abgott*, the true God or a false God.

The Reformer also understood clearly the Christian way to knowledge of the true God. "God has no divinity," he said, "where there is not faith." [1] Faith meant to him an actual person-to-person encounter whereby a man stands *coram Deo*, in God's presence, and responds to him with one's whole being in an I-Thou relationship. Without such an encounter, "instead of the true and natural God, men worship the dreams and imaginations of their

---

[1] *Weimarer Ausgabe* of Luther's works, hereafter designated as *W.A.*, 40, 1, 360.

own heart." [2] I have true faith in God "when I not only believe that what is said about Him is true, but put my trust in Him, surrender myself to Him and make bold to deal with Him." [3] But since it is only with the God who confronts me in Christ that I can have such a living encounter and such personal dealings, "I should not and I will not know of any other God except him who is in my Lord Christ." [4]

I know no better guide to a theological discussion of the nature of God than the man whom we have quoted, for as a leading authority on his thought has said, "Luther's conception of God is not only the most dynamic and definite one but also the most profound and clear one ever produced by Christian theology." [5] But Luther did not invent this approach to God. He rediscovered it in the gospel after long and agonizing years of exploration had shown him the futility of all human attempts to penetrate the secret place of the Most High. It is implicit in the nature of the Word as God's outreach for man, a constant invitation to meet God. The Bible is not a record of man's quest for God. Its keynote is struck in its opening words, "In the beginning God." God himself is first, and faith has objective content only as a response to him. The Bible therefore is not concerned with arguments about God's existence. It leaves such speculation to fools[6] and demons.[7] God's presence surrounds us on all sides, and one who is sensitive to it knows no place to flee from it. His pertinent question is how to become qualified to stand in God's presence and enter into a right relation to him. It is the quality of a man's whole life that is involved, not only his opinions and feelings. "Blessed are the pure in heart, for they shall see God." [8] Knowledge of God is therefore not a matter of intellectual curiosity

[2] *Commentary on Galatians*, Middleton tr., London, 1839, p. 319.
[3] *Works*, Holman edition, II, p. 368.
[4] *W.A.*, 28, 100.
[5] E. Hirsch, *Luthers Gottesanschauung*.
[6] Ps. 53:1.   [7] Jas. 2:19.   [8] Matt. 5:8.

or wishful thinking but of the will[9] and of conscience.[10] God addresses each man as an individual "thou" and calls him to give an account of himself in terms of personal responsibility. It is only when a man's total existence has thus been placed in the light of God's countenance, his secret sins exposed, and his vain pretensions shattered, that an honest personal relation to God becomes possible. A man discovers to his amazement and joy that the purpose of God's search for him has been not only to judge but also to redeem. A new life with God begins on the basis of God's grace and man's gratitude.

This evangelical insight into the way in which true knowledge of God is obtained shows how deeply the stewardship idea of a responsible personal relation between God and man is rooted in divine revelation. Of basic importance is the implication that God himself must be conceived as a person. If faith is an encounter between person and person, where one person speaks and another responds, one person acts and another reacts, then the personality of God is a self-evident presupposition. It is as unnecessary to demonstrate it as it is to argue that God exists. What God is in himself, apart from the encounter of faith, we cannot say. He is a *Deus absconditus*, a terrifying hidden majesty whose depths we cannot fathom. "Who has known the mind of God?" But the God who seeks us in the person of Christ and reveals to us both his mind and his heart cannot be less than a person. Some impersonal principle of cosmic or social integration may be adequate for a religion of rational speculation or mystical absorption. But life in fellowship with God, in prayer and worship, in trust and obedience, in the consecrated loyalty of stewardship, demands the living personal God of Christian faith.

From the point of view of stewardship it is important to note the dynamism implied in these personal relations. Here is living action and reaction, stimulus and response, never mere passivity.

[9] John 7:17.   [10] II Cor. 4:2; I Tim. 3:9.

29

God actively seeks, communicates, energizes, and man responds with his life. But it is also important to bear in mind that in this activity it is God who takes the initiative. What man does is always a response to what God does. All varieties of "bootstrap" religion are thus ruled out. Techniques which men cultivate to make their thinking more positive and their attitudes more confident may or may not be good psychology, but they have nothing to do with Christian theology. In self-centered natural religiosity, even when it is given a Christian veneer, man seeks his own peace and happiness and cross-examines God to see whether he can be of use in attaining this end. In the gospel, where the point of contact between God and man is conscience, it is man who is cross-examined by God. Stewardship must take a firm stand on this ground if it is to be genuinely Christian.

When Christian faith is required to define more closely the nature of the God whom it has encountered, it responds first of all: "I believe in God the Father Almighty, Maker of heaven and earth." Faith's primary affirmation is that God is God, the creator and owner of all that exists. The doctrine of creation is not essentially cosmogony or cosmology, a metaphysical explanation of the origin and structure of the world. It is a glorious *Te Deum* in praise of the sovereignty of God. When pretenders rise to challenge his right to the throne of the universe, faith answers: "Lift up your eyes on high and see; who created these? . . . The Lord is the everlasting God, the Creator of the ends of the earth." [11] This is and remains his world. "Behold the heaven and the heaven of heavens is the Lord's thy God, the earth also, with all that therein is." [12] "The earth is the Lord's and the fulness thereof, the world, and those who dwell therein." [13] Creation establishes the right of eminent domain by which he rules over all things. "The sea is his, for he made it"; the earth is his "for his hands formed the dry land," [14] "we are his" because "it is he

[11] Isa. 40:20-28.   [12] Deut. 10:14, A.V.   [13] Ps. 24:1.   [14] Ps. 95:5.

that made us." [15] This truth, so fundamental to Old Testament revelation, not only retains its validity in the New Testament but deepens and broadens. "O the depth of the riches and wisdom and knowledge of God," exclaims Paul, "for from him and through him and to him are all things. To him be glory forever." [16]

The emphasis on divine sovereignty is the majestic undertone of the theology of the Reformation. It was developed with uncompromising thoroughness in the imposing system constructed by John Calvin. The role which it plays in Luther's thought is hardly less important. Its significance for the everyday devotion of ordinary Christians is clearly stated in the familiar words of the explanation of the first article of the Creed in the Small Catechism and in the less familiar explanation of the first commandment in the Large Catechism, where the Reformer defines God as the object "in which the heart puts all its trust" and warns especially against assuming that attitude toward money. *The Bondage of the Will*, upon which contemporary Luther research has focused so much attention, is unsurpassed in its emphasis on the absoluteness of God's sovereignty. The first lesson that faith must learn is to give glory to God. He called the world into being out of nothingness, and should he for a moment withdraw his hand from it, it would collapse back into nothingness. Faith lets God be God and gives him the honor that is due to him. Sin, on the other hand, is a crookedness of the spiritual spine, man's bending back upon himself. It is rebellion against God's sovereignty, the setting up of the false god, self, in the place of the true God.

The doctrine of God as the sovereign Creator and Sustainer of all existence is one of the foundation stones of the theology of stewardship. It provides first the right orientation to the material world. In formulating the first article of its creed, faith in the almighty Maker of heaven and earth, the early church raised a

[15] Ps. 100:3.   [16] Rom. 11:33-36.

strong bulwark against the Greek notion, represented by the Gnostics, that the physical order of things is something evil or unsubstantial and that the purpose of religion is to enable man to escape into a world of pure spirituality. This idea finds its classical expression in Plato, to whom the body was only the prison house of the soul and the physical world one of shadows. Plotinus, the Neoplatonist, was so obsessed with the spiritual and the eternal that he blushed with shame when he remembered that he had a body and tried to forget his birthday. This type of religiosity found its way into Christianity and flowered in the monastic otherworldliness of the Middle Ages. It is significant that in putting an end to the artificial distinction between the sacred and the profane spheres of life Luther appealed to the doctrine of creation: "To take care of one's children, to love one's wife, to obey the authorities, these are fruits of the Spirit. Among the papists they are works of the flesh, for they do not understand what creation is." [17] But even among Luther's followers religion is often so spiritualized that it has little contact with the realities of creation. The European pastor who told me that he blushed when following a sermon he had to announce an offering and thus divert the attention of his people from the gospel to material things had much in common with Plotinus.

Such was not the case with the apostle Paul. In the fifteenth chapter of I Corinthians, the Magna Charta of resurrection, he rises to the sublimest heights of supernatural revelation, but in the opening of the sixteenth chapter he proceeds, without any apologies, to speak about an offering for the poor of Jerusalem and to give practical instructions for the raising of funds for the work of the church. It was because the apostle saw that all things were created through and for Christ[18] that he never separated redemption from creation. The goal toward which he looked was not the salvation of souls into pure spirituality but the re-

[17] Quoted in G. Wingren, *Luthers lära om kallelsen* (1942), p. 249n.
[18] Col. 1:16.

demption of all creation from the bondage of corruption to fulfil its God-given purpose.[19] There is nothing in the world which God has created that is independent of him or unrelated to his purpose. As Luther taught in his doctrine of the two regimes, both the realm of spiritual things and the realm of earthly things are under the sovereignty of the Creator. There is a Christian variety of secularism to which nothing created is foreign. It defies compartmentalization. It sets forth God's will in every area of life. It says to the dictator, "You have no right to usurp for yourself the power belonging to God." It says to the miser, "You have no right to hoard for yourself the means God has given for doing his work." This all-embracing application of the truth that God is Lord over his creation is the very nerve of stewardship.

Inseparably connected with the Creator's sovereignty is the idea of *ownership*. It is the Creator's prerogative to declare: "The world and all that is in it is mine";[20] "Every beast of the forest is mine, the cattle on a thousand hills";[21] "The silver is mine, and the gold is mine."[22] If God is God, then man can actually never own anything. Even from a purely secular point of view property is correlated with governing authority. Private property cannot be anything absolute but is held as a grant from the government which guarantees the title, and its value depends on the security afforded by the government. If the government of a country cannot hold in check the forces of lawlessness within its borders or the forces of aggression from without, a citizen cannot hold what he considers to be his own.

In the religious sense all ownership is similarly related to God's government of the world. Scripture recognizes the rebellion that has taken place within creation and defies God's sovereignty. Not only does the sinful self-will of individual man constantly

[19] Rom. 8:21. [20] Ps. 50:12. [21] Ps. 50:10. [22] Hag. 2:8.

33

seek to usurp for itself what belongs to God but it is allied with a demonic power which holds the nations in its grip. "The nations conspire, .. the kings of the earth set themselves . . . against the Lord and his anointed, saying, 'Let us burst their bonds asunder.' " [23] Thus Satan tempts Christ by offering him the kingdoms of this world in all their glory, saying, "for it has been delivered to me." [24] But the gospel sees also the failure of the rebellion. Although the pretender to the divine throne is a heavily armed strong man, apparently unconquerable, a "stronger than he" has come to bind him and to take away from him the goods he has wrongfully acquired. The rebellion is only an episode, for through the work of redemption God's creation reverts for all eternity to its rightful owner. The last word in the cosmic drama is: "The kingdom of the world has become the kingdom of our Lord and of his Christ, and he shall reign for ever and ever." [25]

Recognition of the Creator as sovereign Lord of his creation yields another concept of vital importance to stewardship, namely, the *instrumental* character of material things. The natural world is the work of God's hands, the instrument of his purpose, never an end in itself. To make the instrument into an end, to set the created thing in the place of the Creator, is the essence of idolatry.

The prophetic writer of Isaiah 44 portrays this perversion with scathing irony. A man cuts down a tree and uses half of it to warm himself and to prepare his food, but from the other half he makes a god to worship. Scripture nowhere idealizes poverty as such or condemns wealth as such but it sounds a constant warning against ascribing intrinsic value to material possessions. "A man's life," says our Lord, "does not consist in the abundance of his possessions." [26] A man's life consists in fellowship with God. It is a bad bargain to exchange the purpose of life for the means of livelihood. "What will it profit a man, if he gains the whole world and forfeits his life?" [27] Jesus was not indifferent to eco-

[23] Ps. 2:1-3.   [24] Luke 4:6.   [25] Rev. 11:15.   [26] Luke 12:15.   [27] Matt. 16:26.

nomic affairs. He did not underrate the importance of bread. The first issue that he faced as he pondered in the wilderness the meaning of his messiahship was whether the Messiah must above all be able to provide bread for his people. And in teaching us to pray he did not forget the necessity of a petition for daily bread. But he also knew that man does not live by bread alone. Men need God even more than they need bread. The right solution to the bread problem itself rests upon the right relation of men to God. Hence "Seek first his kingdom and his righteousness, and all these things shall be yours as well." [28] This does not deny the importance of "all these things" and become occupied solely with "spiritual" concerns. "Your heavenly Father knows that you need them all," need them to live in the kind of world he created. It does deny them first importance, the sovereignty that belongs to God. "You cannot serve God and mammon." [29] Both communistic economic determinism and capitalistic idolatry of wealth serve the false god mammon. Christian stewardship uses mammon to serve the one true God.

Acknowledgment of the absolute sovereignty of God and of the instrumental nature of the things he has created leads to another basic thought of stewardship, the thought of *responsible trusteeship*. We are neither the lords of creation nor slaves of "the elemental spirits of the universe" [30] but stewards to whom the Creator and Owner of all things has entrusted what belongs to him for the realization of his purpose with regard to it. He commits to us the whole world of nature saying, "Fill the earth and subdue it; and have dominion . . . over every living thing that moves upon the earth." [31] But one to whom has been entrusted the property of another is accountable to the owner. Human existence is thus responsible existence. "To whom much is given, of him will much be required." [32] That a correct understanding of the doctrine of creation culminates in a heightened

[28] Matt. 6:33.   [29] Matt. 6:24.   [30] Col. 2:8.   [31] Gen. 1:28   [32] Luke 12:48.

sense of responsibility is well portrayed in the closing words of Luther's explanation of the first article of the Creed: "For all of which I am in duty bound to thank, praise, serve and obey him." Stewardship becomes a philosophy of life which determines not only religious activity in the narrow sense but also all of life's orders: home, citizenship, business and industry, science, art, and education. Everything God has created has a meaning and a purpose based on his will. Physical health, mental capacities, time, opportunity, daily occupation, material possessions—all these must be viewed as talents which God has entrusted to us to use according to his purpose.

The word which Luther uses to describe this stewardship of all earthly reality is vocation (*vocatio, Beruf*). The centrality of this concept in the Reformer's theology is one of the discoveries of the intensive Luther research of the present century. To Nygren it ranks with *sola fide*, by faith alone, and *simul justus et peccator*, sinner and saint at the same time, as one of the three basic insights of the Reformation.[33] According to Prenter, Luther's teaching on vocation brings to light what is essential and central in his understanding of the gospel.[34] The Swedish theologians, notably Billing and Wingren, have explored this teaching most fully. In the light of these studies we now see that vocation to Luther was not a detachable appendix to the fundamental doctrine of justification by grace nor a romantic notion of regarding the workshop as a church. It interprets and applies concretely to life all the basic themes of Luther's theology, God and man, the law and the gospel, faith and love, creation and redemption. The roots of the idea of vocation are in the doctrine of creation. God, the creator of life, gives every man his occupation, his place in the divine economy. His will confronts us in the concrete tasks of everyday life. This applies to all men,

---

[33] *Svensk teologisk kvartalsskrift* (1947), p. 105.
[34] *Spiritus Creator* (Philadelphia: Muhlenberg Press, 1953), p. 300.

Christians and non-Christians alike. Whether they are believers or not, the father who provides for his children, the ruler who protects his subjects, and the cobbler who makes shoes for people to wear—all are serving God. Vocation refers to the earth, not to heaven. It is not directed upward to God, but outward toward one's fellow-man. It has nothing to do with salvation, justification, the winning of eternal life. These belong to the realm of the gospel where everything is the free gift of grace. Vocation belongs to the realm of the law, God's rule over his earthly kingdom. As such it has a coercive character utterly foreign to the gospel. By his law, operating in the orders of creation and the occupations inherent in them, God compels even godless men to serve one another and thus restrains the powers of evil which would otherwise destroy his creation.

While vocation is thus coextensive with all of life and not an exclusively Christian concept, it is only the Christian man who is aware of his earthly occupation as a divine calling. In the light of the gospel he sees the love of God at work beneath the harsh coercion of the law. While his daily work appears to have nothing to do with God, he sees it as a mask disguising God's presence. He recognizes the world with all its activities as God's workshop, not something neutral, secular, or profane, to which the church must try to give spiritual content. He learns to avoid a false division between the spiritual and the earthly, faith and works, love of God and love of neighbor. "In faith we rise into the presence of God to appropriate as a gift, without works, the gospel, justification, free conscience, and heaven. But within faith there is always a double movement which means that we at once return down to earth, to men, to vocation. Works are swept out of heaven to the earth where the neighbor alone is the center of everything." [35] God's call comes to us in our neighbor's need. When a man runs away from his fellow-man to cultivate

[35] E. Niinivaara, *Maallinen ja Hengellinen* (Helsinki: 1952), p. 27.

37

his own relation to God, he does not find God but only his own worthless self. The outward movement whereby the faith that has risen to God is transformed into works of love is to Luther a duplication of the miracle of the incarnation. Like Christ, faith comes down from heaven to earth to love and to serve. As God came to us not in his naked majesty but clothed in the lowly garb of his Suffering Servant, so God continues to come to earth through his servants who fulfil their earthly obligations in obedient love.

Since a Christian is a citizen of two worlds, the new world of redemption and the old world of creation, the exercise of the life of faith within the earthly vocation involves constant tension and daily crucifixion of the "old man." The "new man" serves his fellow-man with a joy and a spontaneity unknown to those who know only the compulsion of the law. A believer is free to devote all his efforts to this earthly service, for the salvation he has received as a gift makes his efforts unnecessary in the context of heaven. But to the old sinful nature, which clings even to a Christian, the menial tasks of the mundane vocation are a cross and a burden. There is a temptation to identify the cause of God's kingdom with church activities and to separate it from the dull drudgery of daily work. It is easier to bear witness to one's faith by testifying at a religious meeting than by attending more conscientiously to the duties at the office or by being more patient in caring for one's sick mother.[36] God's sovereignty extends over all creation, and every task which he entrusts to us within it has divine significance. We attest the genuineness of our faith by doing whatever he gives us to do with joy and gratitude.

One other aspect of the doctrine of creation, one with a profound bearing upon stewardship, requires specific attention. It is this: the sovereignty of the Creator is the *sovereignty of love.*

[36] *Ibid.,* p. 32.

The first article of the Creed confesses faith not only in the almighty Maker and Owner of heaven and earth but in the *Father* almighty. Fatherly love is the distinctive trait of the God of the gospel. Jesus taught us to address the divine Majesty, whose very name devout Jews dreaded to mention, as "Our Father" and to approach him as "dear children their affectionate parent." Observe a loyal and devoted father in his relation to his children, his deep sense of responsibility, unswerving hope and trust, endless patience, and transforming forgiveness, and you know how God feels toward us; you have your best clue to the nature of God. In the story of the prodigal son our Lord has drawn an unforgettable picture of a God with such features. But the gospel does not allow us to forget that God's love is sovereign love, a divine love that transcends our rational and moral considerations, or to derive the "fatherhood of God and brotherhood of man" without further ado from the doctrine of creation. Human reason can give us an Aristotelian God who sits in solitary splendor contemplating his own perfection and refusing to contaminate himself with the imperfections of the world. It cannot give us a God who runs down the road to embrace one whose associations have been with harlots and swine. The son acknowledges that he has forfeited his natural right to the filial status that is restored to him by a sovereign act of forgiveness. Apart from Christ a sinner confronts not a fatherly God but an offended divine Majesty before whom he can only tremble. It is the glory of the gospel, as Luther saw, to reveal to our amazement that the divine Majesty is "ein Brunnquell eitel Liebe," a fountain of sheer love. God's love manifests its unique sovereign character in the discovery that the almighty Lord of heaven and earth loves me, a sinner, and seeks personal fellowship with me. Faber's hymn "My God, how wonderful Thou art" portrays this well:

> "Yet I may love Thee too, O Lord!
> Almighty as Thou art,

For Thou hast stooped to ask of me
The love of my poor heart."

It is obvious that the fatherhood of God obtains its true Christian meaning only when creation and redemption are seen in their inseparable unity. It is God the Maker of heaven and earth who so loved the world that he gave his only Son to redeem it. Through the redeeming work of Christ our filial relation to God is restored and we receive adoption as sons. Leaving to the following chapter a fuller discussion of the theology of redemption, let us observe here two important stewardship implications of the truth that the Creator is our Father. First, in the light of God's fatherhood, the relation to God upon which stewardship rests is far more than trusteeship or vocational service. We are sons and heirs, not merely trustees and servants. We acknowledge with the apostle "You are not your own" [37] and "whether we live or whether we die, we are the Lord's," [38] but the ownership is not the relationship between master and slave. It is the deeper personal relation whereby a father calls his children his own, and a lover calls his beloved his own. Thus also the property entrusted to our care is, in the deepest sense, not another's but our own. The household which a Christian steward manages is his Father's house, hence his own house. Stewardship thus loses its cold legal character and becomes a family affair, a partnership between father and son in the realization of a shared purpose.

When on the basis of our filial relation to God we see our stewardship, not as an administration of something external to us, but as a sharing in God's own life, we learn a second important stewardship lesson; the source and nature of Christian *giving*. If as God's children we are to share in his purpose, then what we do is determined by what he does. Our management of his household is patterned on the way in which he manages it. God's relation to his world is revealed in the heart of the gospel: "God

[37] I Cor. 6:19.   [38] Rom. 14:8.

so loved the world that he gave." As absolute owner of the universe God is not a Shylock who hoards what he has and harshly demands his pound of flesh. He is a loving father who holds nothing back from his children. "If you, then, which are evil, know how to give good gifts to your children, how much more will the heavenly Father . . .?"[39] To give and to keep on giving is the essential nature of God who is love. Love can never be close-lipped or tightfisted. It is impelled by the very character of its being to impart, to share, to sacrifice, to give. Christian giving can therefore never be an occasional performance or a special ceremony. It is the normal, steady, and increasing outflow of life in God.

The motives used to get people to give are manifold. Usually the appeal is to the altruistic impulses of human nature. Give not until it hurts but until it stops hurting and you derive the satisfaction of having made a contribution to a good cause. But human nature being what it is, it is hard to get rid of the hurt unless the giving serves also the purpose of self-interest. Be considerate of others because the life you save may be your own. An Indiana farmer whose cornfield was of the finest was asked why he generously gave seed corn to his neighbors. "It was not because I was generous," he replied, "but because pollen from my neighbors' poor fields was corrupting my corn. I had to do it to protect my own field." Support of the church because it makes the community a better place to live in often rests on a similar basis. Social respectability is also involved. The words "in consideration of the gifts of others" appearing on many a pledge card appeal to the desire to keep up with the Joneses. A psychiatrist looks still deeper and finds the reason for giving in an emotional urge which he analyzes as sublimated guilt feeling. By helping the other fellow you relieve your own sense of guilt.

Although these motives are not unknown among Christian

[39] Luke 11:13.

people, they are irrelevant to Christian giving. In Christian stewardship the nature of giving is derived solely from God's own nature and from our relation to him. All pride of achievement is ruled out by the acknowledgment: "Of thy own have we given thee." [40] The behavior of God's children is shaped by the unconditioned and overflowing love of their Father who "makes his sun rise on the evil and the good, and sends rain on the just and the unjust." [41] This means that they "do good, . . . expecting nothing in return." [42] Giving is supremely exemplified in God's gift of his Son and our Lord's complete giving of himself. "You know the grace of our Lord Jesus Christ, that though he was rich, yet for your sake he became poor, so that by his poverty you might become rich." [43] The Lord who gave himself for us 100 per cent sets up as the measure of giving "not how much we give, but how much we keep back for ourselves." [44] Thus he commends not the rich who gave much and had much left but the poor widow who gave little but gave until there was nothing left.[45] Giving like that needs no law for it is impelled by love that fulfils and more than fulfils the law. It may be guided by such considerations as the tithe, firstlings, and Paul's suggestions to the Corinthian Christians about regular and proportionate contributions,[46] but it is not bound by any of these. Its only governing principle is: "Freely ye have received, freely give." [47] It is a joyful and spontaneous expression of gratitude for what God has given. "God loves a cheerful giver," not one who gives "reluctantly and under compulsion," [48] for God himself "gives to all men generously and without reproaching." [49] Christian giving thus mirrors faithfully the nature of God and the nature of Christian stewardship.

[40] I Chron. 29:14.　[41] Matt. 5:45.　[42] Luke 6:35.　[43] II Cor. 8:9.
[44] V. S. Azariah, *Christian Giving* (New York: Association Press, 1955), p. 61.　[45] Mark 12:41-44.　[46] I Cor. 16:2.　[47] Matt. 10:8, A.V.　[48] II Cor. 9:7.　[49] Jas. 1:5.

CHAPTER IV

Stewardship and Christ

The God of Christian stewardship is "God in Christ." Our study of the Word of God and of the nature of God has already disclosed the radical Christ-centeredness of the theology based on the gospel. Christ is God's revelation of himself and "bears the very stamp of his nature." [1] Without Christ, we like the men of Athens would worship an unknown God. In Christ is all the God we know, but what we know in him is enough, for "in him the whole fulness of deity dwells bodily." [2] The personal fellowship with God which Christian faith offers is based on the central fact of the incarnation. God shares the life of man in order that man may share the life of God. But since man's separation from God is due not only to his creaturely finiteness but to his sin, the work of the incarnate God is essentially the work of redemption. "God was in Christ reconciling . . ." [3] The partnership with God signified by stewardship is based upon the restoration of a filial relation to God through the forgiveness of sins, and its deepest motivation is the joy of redemption. This cannot be expressed better than in the words of Luther's explanation of what faith in Christ means: "I believe that Jesus Christ . . . is my Lord; who has redeemed me, a lost and condemned creature, . . . in order that I might be his, live under him in his kingdom, and serve him in everlasting righteousness, innocence and blessedness." [4] The fact that God's dealings with mankind are mediated by the redeeming God-man is itself stewardship in its most sublimated sense. Paul describes God's eternal plan of redemption as an *oikonomia*, stewardship, entrusted for administration to Christ, God's supreme steward.[5]

[1] Heb. 1:3.   [2] Col. 2:9.   [3] II Cor. 5:19.
[4] *Small Catechism*, Part II, "The Creed."   [5] Eph. 1:5-10.

In presenting the work of Christ, evangelical theology since the days of the Reformation has used the pattern of the three offices: prophet, priest, and king. As prophet Christ reveals to us the will of God. As priest he sacrifices himself for us and atones for our sins. As king he exercises the sovereign lordship which God gave him in putting all things under his feet. This is a useful pattern to follow in studying the relation between stewardship and Christ.

THE PROPHET

Contrary to popular usage, the word *prophet* does not refer primarily to one who is preoccupied with the future. A prophet is a forthteller rather than a foreteller. He is a man inspired by God to be his spokesman, to set forth his will whether it concerns the past, the present, or the future. The Greeks applied the term *prophetes* even to poets who interpreted the divine meaning of life, a usage recognized in the New Testament.[6] The usual scriptural connotation refers to the remarkable succession of God's messengers in the Old Testament, from Moses to John the Baptist, who were inspired to speak or to write in his name. It was as such a figure that Jesus appeared on the scene of history, declaring, "The Spirit of the Lord is upon me . . . He has sent me."[7] The title of prophet was applied to him by the masses of people,[8] by the disciples,[9] and by himself.[10] To Christian faith Jesus is more than a prophet. He is the incarnate Son of God, very God of very God. His teachings are inseparable from his person and his redemptive work. The prophetic office enables us, however, to focus attention upon his role as "a teacher come from God." It is in this context, then, that we may deal most appropriately with those teachings of our Lord that have a specific bearing on stewardship.

[6] Titus 1:12.   [7] Luke 4:18.
[8] Matt. 14:5; Matt. 21:46; Luke 7:16.
[9] Luke 24:19.   [10] Matt. 13:57; Luke 13:33.

44

Jesus' teachings provide exceedingly rich material for the interpretation of the meaning of life in terms of stewardship. The central theme of his proclamation, the kingdom of God, is neither a moral ideal nor a social hope. It is precisely that eternal sovereignty of God over all existence which we have already seen to be the keynote of the theology of stewardship. Our Lord presents the kingdom in the double aspect of a present reality, a new age inaugurated by his own coming, and a future consummation, the complete fulfilment of God's purpose. Wherever the kingdom touches man's present existence it contains stewardship implications. Our summary of them can afford to be quite brief both because they have already been quite fully discussed in other stewardship studies and because the Christ-centered nature of the present study involves our Lord's teachings at every point.

As prophetic revealer of the will of God, Jesus teaches us, first of all, that life obtains its true meaning and purpose when it becomes a wholehearted response to God in obedience and love. Stewardship as an all-embracing life attitude is nowhere more fully and accurately defined than in the "great and first commandment" in which our Lord sees the entire substance of the Law and the Prophets: "You shall love the Lord your God with all your heart, and with all your soul, and with all your strength, and with all your mind; and your neighbor as yourself." [11] Here is a summary of God's claim upon man's total existence, love as the motive for responding to that claim, and human relations as the field in which the response is to be made. As a concrete illustration of such life in action Jesus goes on to tell the story of the good Samaritan. The priest and the Levite represent a self-centered legalistic religiosity in which a man proceeds from the point of view of his own faith and strives for his own holiness. They act strictly according to the letter of the law in seeking to avoid defiling themselves by touching a

[11] Luke 10:27; Matt. 22:37-40.

45

person presumed to be dead. The Samaritan forgets himself and disregards all religious regulations. He acts solely from the point of view of the neighbor's need. Like the Father in heaven who lets his sun rise on the evil and the good, he places all his resources at the disposal of the battered stranger on the road, whoever he may be. He does not have the necessary medicines but he uses what he has, oil and wine. He has no stretcher for carrying the half-dead man, so the donkey has to do. No hospital is at hand, so the nearest inn must serve. He does not have enough money to pay the innkeeper but he gives all he has and says, "I shall owe you the rest." This is our Lord's conception of stewardship.

Love that rises to the occasion so spontaneously and pours itself out so unreservedly has its source in God. It is not a fruit that human nature as such can produce. The figs of self-sacrifice are not gathered from the thistles of self-centeredness. First make the tree good, first change the whole quality of life from within. The heart of our Lord's message is that this transformation is now possible, for the kingdom of God is at hand, a new humanity has begun, new life is being offered as a divine gift. The one and only requirement for entrance into the kingdom, hence the basic prerequisite of the life of stewardship, is the readiness to receive what God has to offer. It is the sensitive receptivity characteristic of childhood that the Lord commends in saying, "Unless you turn and become like children, you will never enter the kingdom of heaven." [12] In the Beatitudes he describes it as poverty of spirit, as acute concern over that poverty, as hungering and thirsting after righteousness, as meekness that depends utterly upon God. The divine gift must be received with "an honest and good heart," with a willingness to lose the old life to find the new. The kingdom is the one priceless pearl for the sake of which a man must be prepared to let every-

[12] Matt. 18:3.

thing else go. The Galilean fishermen who "left everything and followed him" were ready to do this. The rich young man who "went away sorrowful, for he had great possessions" was not. Wholehearted acceptance of the new life is particularly difficult for one who has acquired wealth. "It is easier for a camel to go through the eye of a needle than for a rich man to enter the kingdom of God." [13] Unless riches, together with all of life, are subjected to the stewardship of the kingdom, they carry the danger of perverting means into ends and leading to the inevitable bankruptcy that results from investing in a false god. When a man has spurned God's invitation by thinking more of his field and his oxen, he will never taste of the true banquet that God meant life to be. The rich fool who laid up treasures for himself but was not rich toward God[14] and the rich glutton who feasted sumptuously every day but at death was reduced to the abject poverty of begging for a drop of water[15] are examples of men who have allowed the deceitfulness of riches to lure them into eternal ruin. Dives received only the passing "good things" of the present life, while Lazarus' receptivity toward God was the channel for endless blessing.

Stewardship begins with the receptive attitude but it does not end there. Our Lord's teaching on the kingdom is far too dynamic to stop with mere passive acceptance. He asks for consecrated action which channelizes what has been received into single-minded, loyal, and dependable service. The stewardship parables all contain this emphasis. "Who then is the faithful and wise steward, whom his master will set over his household to give them their portion of food at the proper time? Blessed is that servant whom his master . . . will find so doing." [16] The servants are put "in charge, each with his work." [17] The talents are given to do business with. They must be returned not merely

---

[13] Mark 10:25. [14] Luke 12:16-21. [15] Luke 16:19-31. [16] Luke 12:42-43.
[17] Mark 13:34.

intact but with interest.[18] Even the dishonest steward is commended for his alertness.[19] The kingdom is a vineyard and the call into it is a call to work.[20] The Lord defines his own life mission with the words: "My food is to do the will of him who sent me, and to accomplish his work." [21] He expects of his people the same investment of life in obedience to the Father's will. "Follow me," he says, and "as the Father has sent me, even so I send you." [22] When he speaks of receiving the kingdom as a little child he turns sharply to speak of receiving in another sense, receiving children in his name and performing constructive service in their behalf.[23] The kingdom is more than thinking the right thoughts and speaking the right words. "Not every one who says to me, 'Lord, Lord,' shall enter the kingdom of heaven, but he who does the will of my Father who is in heaven." [24]

One other emphasis in our Lord's teaching on stewardship needs to be pointed out, namely, the steward's responsibility. "To whom much is given, of him will much be required." [25] This is the central thought of the stewardship parables. The entrusted talents must be accounted for. The master of the household will return at an unknown hour expecting every servant to be at his assigned post. The steward who used his master's property for his own ends will be punished. Our Lord's message is never merely sweetness and light. The thought of judgment is always present as a solemn undertone. Even that glorious gospel in miniature, John 3:16, contains the grim word "perish." The genuineness of the faith which appropriates God's gift of eternal life will be tested by the works of love performed to the little brethren.

The steward's responsibility includes the responsibility to be intelligent. We must be as wise as serpents as well as innocent as doves. The rich farmer with the bursting barns, the man who

---

[18] Matt. 25:14-30.   [19] Luke 16:8.   [20] Matt. 20:1-16.   [21] John 4:34.
[22] John 20:21.   [23] Matt. 18:5-6.   [24] Matt. 7:21.   [25] Luke 12:48.

built his house on the sand, the virgins whose lamps lacked oil—these people are not condemned for their wickedness but for their stupidity. Stewardship as intelligence, as loving God with all one's mind, finds its most remarkable expression in the story of the dishonest steward.[26] Since this story both sums up our Lord's basic teaching on stewardship and makes a realistic application of it to everyday life, we may conclude the present section of our study by examining it more closely. If the story is regarded as a parable and the lord who called his steward to account represents God, it is difficult to explain why God should commend the dishonest man and place his approval upon a clever piece of cheating. Evidently we have here not a parable but an incident from life showing how smart but godless businessmen have gone about their business in all ages. But just as a bee extracts honey even from a poisonous flower, so our Lord draws important lessons from the sinful conduct of the worldly-wise.

First is the lesson that life is a stewardship. The dishonest steward did not own anything. All that he had belonged to his lord and was only entrusted to his administration for use in the best interest of the owner. Our situation is the same. What we have, our material possessions, our mental talents and abilities, our time and energy, our potentialities and opportunities, it is all a trust for which we are obligated to God and accountable to him. The second lesson is that we face a day of reckoning. We confront not a mere principle of retribution but the judgment throne of God himself. The dishonest steward wasted his lord's goods, appropriating for his own use property which was not his. He seemed to get away with it and laughed at pious talk of responsibility, but the day came when he heard the abrupt and appalling summons, "Turn in the account of your stewardship." In using for our own selfish pleasure the resources which God has given to do the work of his kingdom we too are guilty of embezzlement.

[26] Matt. 20:28.

Our Lord declares that we cannot get away with this highhanded-
ness. God will not be mocked. We are under his judgment. At
any moment we must be prepared to turn in the account of our
stewardship.

The main point of the story comes in the third lesson: we
must be intelligent enough to insure the future. The dishonest
steward was quick to act when the crisis came. He called his
lord's debtors and by arbitrarily changing their notes and altering
their indebtedness he made them his partners in crime. He obligated them to himself in such a way as to be able to turn to them
when he was deposed from office. Our Lord does not commend
the man's rascality but he does say that the man acted intelligently
according to the low standards which he had chosen. He insured
his temporary earthly future. But we, concludes the Lord, must
be just as intelligent and alert to insure our future according to
the high standards which he has given us. With eternal habita-
tions in mind we must make friends by means of "unrighteous
mammon."

Here is a superb example of the realistic wisdom of the Prophet
of Galilee. High objectives, a right attitude, and a strong sense
of responsibility are not enough for the conduct of life. They
must be implemented with intelligent procedures. We must know
how to act in concrete situations, otherwise we shall cast our
pearls before swine and give that which is holy to dogs. The
children of light must not allow the children of this world to
have a monopoly on wisdom. Mammon must be put to use, a
use that is wise as well as just. The mammon which we must
handle for righteous purposes is unrighteous. Jesus, the supreme
realist, sees that in a sin-cursed world our stewardship must be
carried out through sin-tainted decisions and with sin-tainted instruments. Indeed, the steward himself, as Luther observed, is
sinner and saint, righteous and unrighteous, at the same time.
But living by the grace of forgiveness by which our Judge is

also our Savior, we fulfil our calling according to the wisdom and the strength which he gives us.

THE PRIEST

The Christ of the Christian faith is more than a prophet. He is the High Priest who laid down his life on the altar of the Cross to redeem us from sin and death. He defines the central purpose of his mission thus: "The Son of man came . . . to give his life as a ransom for many." The church responds: "The reason the Son of God appeared was to destroy the works of the devil";[27] he "obtained eternal redemption for us." [28] Redemption presupposes that man is a sinner and as such he is cut off from God. Through sin we have lost the right to divine sonship and the power to carry out the tasks growing out of that sonship. The gospel is the good news that the Revealer of the will of God is also the Redeemer. God himself has engaged in a triumphant saving action to overcome man's sin and in his sovereign grace establishes fellowship with man on the basis of forgiveness. Those who accept the gospel of forgiveness in faith receive the power to become not only God's trustees but also his children. The motive for their action is grateful love. The more livingly we know him who loved us and gave himself for us the more completely we give ourselves to him. And because genuine love is "not in word, neither in tongue, but in deed and in truth," [29] we shoulder the responsibilities of Christian stewardship. This theme threads through our entire study and its specific application to the individual Christian believer will be discussed in chapter VI. The present task is to present a concise objective summary of the meaning which the doctrine of the atonement has for stewardship.

In the gospel by which the church lives and the theology based upon it, the death of Christ on the cross has always had central importance. Paul defines the whole substance of the gospel as

[27] I. John 3:8.   [28] Heb. 9:12, A.V.   [29] I John 3:18, A.V.

"the word of the cross." [30] He is therefore determined "to know nothing . . . except Jesus Christ and him crucified." [31] The richness of meaning which the gospel ascribes to the crucifixion is reflected in the variety of words which it uses in describing it: atonement, expiation, propitiation, redemption, sacrifice, reconciliation, salvation, victory. The church's attempt through the centuries to fathom the meaning of the cross has resulted in a corresponding variety of interpretations, some superficial, others profound, each serving as a facet of inexhaustible truth. All this theology may appear at first to have little to do with that practical and applied Christianity which we call stewardship. Yet the intimate connection between the two is clearly stated by the greatest of the theologians of the cross: "For the love of Christ controls us, because we are convinced that one has died for all . . . that those who live might live no longer for themselves but for him who for their sake died and was raised." [32] The fundamental stewardship emphases "the love of Christ controls us" and "we live for him" are rooted in a firm conviction of the truth of the theological affirmation "One died for all." Without clear and positive Christian convictions there can be no vital Christian stewardship. This is particularly true of the central doctrine of Christ's atoning death. A man will not make the full surrender of his life to Christ demanded by stewardship unless he knows that Christ died for him.

One interpretation of the crucifixion is quite easy to understand. It is the view that Jesus was a uniquely God-conscious and consecrated man and his death a supreme example of his own stewardship. Thus Knudson, following a line of thought which stems from Schleiermacher, attaches primary importance to the fact that Jesus as revealer of God "was unswervingly faithful to his divine vocation" and that "it was faithfulness to this vocation

[30] I Cor. 1:18.   [31] I Cor. 2:2.   [32] II Cor. 5:14-15.

52

that led him to the cross." [33] The truth in this view is contained in Paul's description of the Crucified as "obedient unto death, even death on a cross." [34] It is supported by the resoluteness with which Jesus set his face toward Jerusalem where death awaited him, his dedicated "nevertheless not my will, but thine, be done" of Gethsemane, and above all by the perfect goodness manifested in his conduct on the cross. In striking contrast to the cruelty, the godlessness and the spiritual blindness of his enemies, the Man on the cross is everything that God expects man to be. He not only remains sinless, refusing to pit violence against violence, hate against hate, but he answers hate with love. He lifts up the shield of intercession to protect his crucifiers from the divine judgment they deserve. Here then is the truest, the best, the most divine that we know, the worthiest of examples for us to follow.

This interpretation is true as far as it goes but it does not go far enough. It forgets that the vocation to which Jesus was faithful unto death was not only to reveal God but to reconcile men with God. It disregards the context of Paul's reference to the obedient Christ; that he is the sovereign Lord, coequal with God, who assumed the form of a servant to carry out God's redeeming purpose for mankind. His death was not merely that of a man who remained good even though it cost him his life, but that of the Mediator who was "delivered up according to the definite plan and foreknowledge of God." [35] Because of the superficial view of sin on which it rests, this view has an inadequate conception of the Mediator. It makes of Christ little more than a martyr. It has no genuine hope for those who fail to measure up to his lofty example. Of this failure all men are guilty.

The nature of our task does not permit us to enter in detail

[33] *The Doctrine of Redemption* (New York: Abingdon, 1933), pp. 339, 383.
[34] Phil. 2:8.　[35] Acts 2:33.

into the more profound and more difficult theology of the cross, which recognizes the gravity of sin and the immeasurable greatness of the reconciling work performed by the atoning High Priest. Since sin involves both guilt to be expiated and enslaving power to be overcome, this theology moves along two main lines. The first presents the Reconciler in terms of expiatory sacrifice, vicarious suffering, and penal substitution. The second presents the Redeemer whose mighty victory delivers men from the power of evil.

The first is the main line of scriptural revelation. Its roots are deep in the Old Testament. Through the law God reveals not only his holy will but also the distance that separates sinful man from him. Thus already at Sinai, where God establishes a covenant with Israel on the basis of the law, Moses sprinkles the "blood of the covenant" upon the people to symbolize the expiation needed when the law is violated. Through the whole sacrificial system Israel is constantly reminded that without the shedding of blood there is no salvation. The symbolism rises to its climax in the annual Day of Atonement when the high priest entered the holiest of holies and sprinkled the blood of the sacrificial animal upon the mercy seat, the lid of the ark of the covenant, in which the tablets of the law were kept. *Kippur*, the Hebrew word for atonement, has the literal meaning of *covering* and implies the interposing of the innocent sacrificial victim between the righteous wrath of God and the offender. Prophecy at its highest level presents the Messiah himself as the vicarious sacrifice, the lamb led to the slaughter. "He was wounded for our transgressions, . . . upon him was the chastisement that made us whole, . . . the Lord has laid on him the iniquity of us all." [36]

It is in this light that the New Testament views the death of Christ. Our Lord himself portrays his death as the pouring out of the "blood of the covenant" [37] and as the fulfilment of the

[36] Isa. 53. [37] Mark 14:24.

prophecy concerning the vicarious suffering of the Messiah.[88] In the Fourth Gospel John the Baptist calls Jesus "the Lamb of God, who takes away the sin of the world." [39] The Epistle to the Hebrews describes in great detail the fulfilment of the sacrificial system in Christ, "the high priest of the good things that have come," who "once for all . . . put away sin by the sacrifice of himself." [40] In Paul all this light of divine revelation comes to a sharp focus: "One has died for all;" [41] "Christ redeemed us from the curse of the law, having become a curse for us";[42] "For our sake he made him to be sin who knew no sin." [43] This interpretation of the meaning of the crucifixion, expressed later by Anselm in terms of feudal justice and by the Reformers as a conciliation between God's righteousness and God's love, is the very backbone of evangelical theology.

What bearing does this theology of the expiatory, vicarious, and substitutionary character of the death of Christ have upon stewardship? We have already observed that Paul makes the truth "One has died for all" the basis of the Christ-controlled life of stewardship. We have here, first of all, a supreme illustration of the fact that our stewardship does not originate with what we do for God but in a response to what God does for us. What God does in Christ in reconciling the world to himself does not depend on anything that he sees in us, our faith, our penitence, or our obedience. "While we were yet sinners Christ died for us." [44] God's love for sinners is not conditioned by what sinners are like but solely by what God is like. Reconciliation is his own unique and sovereign act in which through the sacrifice made on the cross he himself removes the barrier erected by sin and opens for us the way into fellowship with him. The grace

[88] Luke 22:37. Cf. Isa. 53:12.
[39] John 1:29. [40] Heb. 9. [41] II Cor. 5:14. [42] Gal. 3:13. [43] II Cor. 5:21. [44] Rom. 5:8.

of forgiveness becomes ours through faith but it exists before faith and makes faith possible.

Christ's death for sinners reveals furthermore how fellowship between God and man can be established without minimizing either the deadly seriousness of sin or the sovereign righteousness of God. Here the substitutionary view shows greater depth than the view which concentrates on Christ as the mighty conquerer who breaks down the strongholds of evil and sets the captives free. Sinners need not only to be delivered from bondage to the devil but also to be reconciled with the God against whom they have sinned. Charles Wesley brings out the point well: "He breaks the power of *canceled* sin, He sets the prisoner free." Unless the guilt of sin is canceled there can be no true deliverance.

It is extremely superficial theology to say that God hates sin but loves the sinner. Sin is inseparable from the sinner; it is the sinner himself in action. Thus the scriptural teaching on the atonement stresses throughout the righteous wrath of God which rests upon sinners themselves and which Christ bore in our stead. This is the meaning of Paul's words. God "condemned sin in the flesh" by "sending his own Son in the likeness of sinful flesh and for sin . . . in order that the just requirement of the law might be fulfilled." [45] When our Lord cried out from the depth of his agony, "My God, my God, why hast thou forsaken me?" he tasted for us the very torments of the damned. The cross reveals God in the full sovereignty both of his holiness and of his love. The blessed fellowship with him which makes the stewardship life possible rests on the acknowledgment: "I am a sinner who does not deserve to be God's child and God's partner, but Christ died for me."

The second main line in the theology of the atonement develops the thought of redemption rather than reconciliation. It presents a mighty conflict of powers, the power of evil which

[45] Rom. 8:3-4.

holds mankind captive and *Christus Victor* who by his death triumphs over evil and sets men free. This point of view too has a strong scriptural foundation. It appears already in the "first gospel," the mysterious word spoken by God to Satan immediately following the fall into sin: "I will put enmity between thee and the woman, and between thy seed and her seed; it shall bruise thy head, and thou shalt bruise his heel." [46] This dark saying becomes clear only in the light of the cross. It speaks of a gigantic warfare between mankind, the seed of woman, and the forces of evil, the seed of the serpent. Paradise will be regained when the seed of woman will produce a second Adam who will stand unwavering against the assaults of the Evil One and conquer him. It will not be an easy victory. The serpent will sting and bruise. The Savior will have to suffer bitter agony. But he will crush the serpent's head and bring deliverance to mankind.

The same great note of triumph sounds in Isaiah 53: "He shall see the fruit of the travail of his soul . . . he shall divide the spoil with the strong." Throughout his ministry, from the temptation experience in the wilderness to his passion, our Lord conceived his mission to be a struggle against the forces opposed to God. He also saw that the means of victory was to be his own death. It was to be the ransom by which men were to be set free from the prison of evil, the grain of wheat from which was to grow the harvest of salvation. "In him we have redemption through his blood," [47] rejoices Paul, for "he has delivered us from the dominion of darkness." [48] In subsequent theology this aspect of the atonement is in the foreground in the Greek fathers, while Western thought stresses guilt and sacrifice. The Reformation, for the most part, follows the Western thought pattern as set by Augustine and Anselm, although Luther's portrayal of sin, death, the devil, the law, and the wrath of God as "tyrants"

[46] Gen. 3:15, A.V.   [47] Eph. 1:7.   [48] Col. 1:13.

overthrown by Christ gives full recognition also to the other view. In our day Bishop Aulén has contended that the ideas of ransom and victory represent the church's primary approach to the work of Christ. They show God to be the subject as well as object in the act of atonement, present Christ's whole life of active obedience to God in inseparable unity with the event of his death, and stress the positive and constructive results of Christ's triumph.

The significance of this approach for stewardship is obvious. We need but recall once more Luther's words: "Christ has redeemed me from sin, death, and the power of the devil in order that I might be his own and serve him." The point of view of redemption supplements but does not supplant that of reconciliation. One-sided emphasis upon the latter can easily lead to preoccupation with impersonal juridic categories, while the idea of redemption as such does not provide adequate insight either into man's guilt or God's righteousness. In both cases the accent falls on God's unfathomable love. It is the underlying motive of reconciliation: "God shows his love for us in that while we were yet sinners Christ died for us." [49] And it is "through him who loved us" that "we are more than conquerors." [50] The triumph which this love achieved for all mankind attains its purpose in us when the "blood of Christ" shall "purify our conscience from dead works to serve the living God." [51] The response which stewardship makes to the love manifest on Calvary is this:

> "Love so amazing, so divine
> Demands my soul, my life, my all."

THE KING

The message which Jesus proclaimed as our Prophet obtains its sovereign authority, and the sacrifice which he made for us

[49] Rom. 5:8. [50] Rom. 8:37. [51] Heb. 9:14.

as our High Priest obtains its validity as the basis of a new relation between God and man, through his being the divinely appointed ruler of all life, the King of kings and the Lord of lords. Christian faith bases the lordship of Christ upon his resurrection from the dead, his triumphant ascension to the right hand of God, and his promise to return in glory to judge the living and the dead. What does this faith in the living and exalted Christ mean for Christian stewardship?

The resurrection of Christ from the dead is the foundation event of the new age which began with him, comparable only to creation when life itself began. It is the event to which the church owes its existence, its message, and its mission. What the New Testament has to say about Christ all proceeds from the conviction that he is the risen and living Lord. His victory over death distinguishes him from all prophets, teachers, and heroes of faith. He was "designated Son of God in power . . . by his resurrection from the dead." [52] The resurrection establishes him as the Mediator of the new covenant who was "raised for our justification." [53] The same "working of his great might which he accomplished in Christ when he raised him from the dead" [54] makes the gospel "the power of God unto salvation." It is by this resurrection power that the church lives and carries out its mission. Its sacraments are an actual communion with the living Lord. Its members "taste of the powers of the world to come," for by his resurrection Christ has brought into the present world the life of the world to come, and faith is access to this life. We "rise with Christ into a newness of life" and become the channels through which this life flows into the world. Thus to pray with Paul that we "may know the power of his resurrection" [55] is to seek the deepest meaning and the richest resources of our stewardship. Significantly enough Luther concludes his explanation of what the work of Christ means to the individual believer

[52] Rom. 1:4.   [53] Rom. 4:25.   [54] Eph. 1:19-20.   [55] Phil. 3:10.

with the words: "that I may serve him . . . even as he is risen from the dead, and lives and reigns to all eternity."

Christ's resurrection is the unique midpoint of history, the end of the dominion of sin and death and the beginning of the reign of the Messiah. It is on the basis of this victory achieved once and for all over the demonic "principalities and powers" that the church affirms triumphantly, "Jesus is Lord." The victory, "he rose again," establishes the lordship, "he ascended into heaven and sitteth on the right hand of God the Father Almighty." It is idle to speculate about the "ascension into heaven" and "the right hand of God" in spatial terms, for the divine majesty of the exalted Lord recognizes no limitations of either space or time. Paul portrays gloriously the true meaning of the exaltation: "He raised him from the dead and made him sit at his right hand in the heavenly places, far above all rule and authority and power and dominion, and above every name that is named, not only in this age but also in that which is to come; and he has put all things under his feet and has made him the head over all things." [56] The apostle goes on to say that God has made Christ head over all things "for the church, which is his body, the fulness of him who fills all in all." [57] The church is the visible center of the rule of him by whom all things were made and who upholds all things by the word of his power. In this light Christian stewardship takes on nothing less than cosmic significance. Its aim is the restoration of all areas of life to its rightful Lord. John Ellerton has captured this insight in the beautiful lines of his hymn:

> "Thine is the loom, the forge, the mart,
> The wealth of land and sea;
> The worlds of science and of art,
> Revealed and ruled by Thee.

[56] Eph. 1:20-22.   [57] Eph. 1:23.

"Then let us prove our heavenly birth
In all we do and know:
And claim the kingdom of the earth
For Thee, and not Thy foe."

The lordship of Christ extends not only over the church but over all creation. It is the church's mission to bear clear witness that to Christ belongs "all authority in heaven and on earth," that every aspect of life obtains its ultimate meaning and purpose only in relation to him. All men already stand under the rule of Christ, whether they acknowledge his lordship or not. This is part of that "manifold wisdom of God" entrusted to the church to be made known through it to "the principalities and powers" of the world.[58] Christian stewards are men and women who have found the true Lord of life and whose words and deeds witness to his lordship.

Trusting Christ's own specific promise,[59] the church affirms finally: "He shall come again with glory to judge both the quick and the dead; whose kingdom shall have no end." With the consummation of God's eternal plan for the world the kingship of Christ will become universally manifest. The truth by which Christians now live, "Jesus Christ is Lord," will then be confessed by every tongue.[60] Far from being fanciful speculation about unknown things, Christ's return in glory is the assured end result of the triumph already achieved in his resurrection. It is the inevitable V-Day, as Cullmann expresses it, which will follow the D-Day of Easter. This assurance of the eventual complete triumph of Christ and his kingdom gives Christian stewardship its deepest perspective, its strongest incentive, and its surest guarantee of ultimate worth. It is the ground of the great "therefore": "Therefore, my beloved brethren, be steadfast, immovable,

[58] Eph. 3:10.
[59] Mark 14:61-62; Matt. 26:63-64; Luke 22:66-69.
[60] Phil. 2:11.

always abounding in the work of the Lord, knowing that in the Lord your labor is not in vain." [61] In the perspective of eternity work in the Lord is the only work with a future. But this assurance also raises to its highest the responsibility with which Christian stewards are charged: "Watch therefore—for you do not know when the master of the house will come, in the evening, or at midnight, or at cockcrow, or in the morning—lest he come suddenly and find you asleep. And what I say to you I say to all: Watch." [62]

[61] I Cor. 15:58.　　[62] Mark 13:35-37.

CHAPTER V

The Holy Spirit and the Church

The distinctive trait of the Christian life is that it is created and sustained by the Holy Spirit. The faith that motivates stewardship, the acceptance of Jesus as the Lord of our whole life and the dedication of all that we are and have to him, is impossible to self-centered human nature. It is the work of the Holy Spirit. "No one," declares Paul, "can say 'Jesus is Lord' except by the Holy Spirit."[1] And Luther begins his explanation of the third article of the Creed with the words: "I cannot by my own reason or strength believe in Jesus Christ my Lord, or come to him; but the Holy Spirit has called me . . . enlightened me . . . sanctified me." Faith, in the Christian sense, differs from all other forms of belief. It is generated by God himself, not by our reason, desire, or will. It is a duplication of the miracle of the incarnation: eternity enters time, God's life enters ours. The Christ who died for us becomes the Christ who lives in us. Through the Holy Spirit the realities of creation, God's sovereignty and our responsibility, and the realities of redemption, the forgiveness of sins and new life in Christ, become vital personal realities. The doctrine of the Spirit is a constant reminder that in true Christian faith and life the initiative belongs to God, that what we do is a response to what he does.

A Christian steward, therefore, is not just a man who has developed an interest in spiritual things as distinguished from worldly things. He is a man who has received the Spirit, is guided by the Spirit, and prays to be filled with the Spirit. The distinction that he makes between spirit and flesh is not between his higher and lower nature but between a right and a wrong

[1] I Cor. 12:3.

relation to God and hence between a right and a wrong use of all things, material as well as spiritual. Apart from the Spirit, the whole man, including his higher pursuits such as morality and religion, is flesh, that is, the self-seeking old Adam that clings even to the most spiritual-minded of men. The new life in God and under God's control is entirely the activity of the Spirit of God.

The richness of the doctrine of the Holy Spirit is evident from the fact that the gospel ascribes to him both the transformation of individual life, the birth and growth of Christian personality, and the creation and preservation of the Christian community, the church. The work of the Spirit in leading individual men to Christ is the subject of the next chapter. The present task is to seek to understand, in their relation to stewardship, the function of the Spirit in the divine *oikonomia* as a whole and the nature of the church as the community of the Spirit.

THE HOLY SPIRIT IN THE DIVINE ECONOMY

"As yet the Spirit had not been given," writes the author of the Fourth Gospel, "because Jesus was not yet glorified." [2] He points thus to a divine plan for the world, which centers in Christ and enables us to see the work of the Spirit in its true perspective. Much of the confusion attending the doctrine of the Holy Spirit may be avoided when his work is placed in the setting of God's redemptive plan which unfolds in history. We thus learn, first of all, to distinguish between human spirituality in its various forms and the Holy Spirit. Idealistic philosophers of all times and climes, Plato in ancient Greece, Sankara in India, Berkeley in Ireland, Hegel in Germany, Royce and Brightman in twentieth-century America, to mention but a few, have sought ultimate reality in a world of the spirit which transcends the physical world but is kin to man's spiritual nature. The mystics of all the

[2] John 7:39.

world religions have developed methods for overcoming the flesh and heightening the spiritual element in man until it makes direct contact with, or is even absorbed in, the cosmic spirit. Imposing systems of morality have been constructed for the purpose of raising men to a higher and more spiritual plane of living. All these efforts toward a spiritualization of life must be recognized for what they are, man's attempts to develop what he regards as the supreme values of existence and to seek cosmic support for them. But they must not be confused with the Holy Spirit whom the crucified and risen Christ, upon his ascension to the glory of his Father, sent to his disciples to perpetuate his own presence in their midst.

In the light of the Christ-centered plan of redemption we learn also to evaluate properly the numerous references to the Spirit in the Old Testament. Beginning with its opening verses,[3] where the Spirit is portrayed as God himself in creative action, the Old Testament throughout presents the Spirit as the Giver of life both to nature in general and to human beings.[4] He equips both the national and the religious leaders of Israel for their tasks[5] and he brings God's own presence into the hearts of the faithful.[6] There is an unbroken continuity between the Spirit in the Old Testament and the New, and the early church retained the identification when it included in the third article of its Creed the words "who spake by the prophets." How, then, are we to solve the apparent contradiction between this view and the equally clear affirmation that the Spirit was not given until Pentecost?

The answer lies in the history of redemption, in which the Old Testament is a preparatory stage and Christ the fulfilment. The God who "in many and various ways . . . spoke of old to our fathers by the prophets" is the same God who "in these last days

[3] Gen. 1:1-2.
[4] Ps. 104:30; Job 34:14-15; Isa. 40:7; Ezek. 37:9-10.
[5] Num. 11:17; Judg. 3:10; I Sam. 11:6; Ezek. 2:2; Mic. 3:8.
[6] Ps. 51:11; Ps. 139:7.

has spoken to us by a Son." [7] The Spirit whom the fathers saw as God in life-giving action in nature, in history, and in individual experience is the same Spirit whom the church of the New Testament sees in a new and clearer light in God's full revelation of himself in Christ. Divine revelation in the Old Testament not only undergoes a progressive clarification but also points beyond itself to a future consummation. The New Testament announces the fulfilment of prophecy, the arrival of a new age of the Spirit which begins with the completion of the work of Jesus.

In the redemptive plan of God the work of the Spirit is inseparably connected with the work of Christ. Already in the Old Testament the Spirit is associated with the promised Messiah: "The Spirit of the Lord shall rest upon him." [8] It was in terms of such a prophecy that Jesus described his mission.[9] And it was to another such prophetic promise that Peter appealed in explaining the meaning of Pentecost.[10] Every phase of our Lord's life and activity is marked by the presence of the Spirit: his birth, his baptism, his temptation, his miracles, his teaching. As the crucifixion approached, he spoke ever more clearly and fully about the coming of "another Counselor" and prepared the disciples to receive him. "Through the eternal Spirit" he made the atoning sacrifice on the Cross,[11] through the Spirit he was raised from the dead,[12] and the Spirit was his resurrection gift to the disciples on Easter night.[13] After the ascension, in obedience to their Lord's instructions, the company of disciples remained together in Jerusalem awaiting the coming of the Spirit which took place on Pentecost.

The keynote of Pentecost is fulfilment. Fulfilled are the prophecies of old, fulfilled is the saving purpose of God which Christ came to carry out. The rebellion against God has been crushed,

[7] Heb. 1:1. [8] Isa. 11:2. [9] Luke 4:18. Cf. Isa. 61:1.
[10] Acts 2:17-21. Cf. Joel 2:28-32.
[11] Heb. 9:14. [12] Rom. 1:4; 8:11. [13] John 20:22.

the Messiah has triumphed. As the result of his victory the power of a new creation now flows into the world, a new age has begun under his lordship, a new humanity has been born of which he is the Head. This was the substance of Peter's sermon on Pentecost. "Being therefore exalted at the right hand of God, and having received from the Father the promise of the Holy Spirit, he has poured out this which you see and hear. . . . God has made him both Lord and Christ, this Jesus whom you crucified." [14] Peter's explanation of the meaning of Pentecost takes the form of a vindication of the resurrection and exaltation of Christ. The sending of the Spirit is incontrovertible proof that the crucified Jesus lives and reigns. Such is the apostolic witness throughout. The Spirit does not take the place of Christ. He leads men to experience Christ as a living reality. The God with whom he affords rich new personal contact is God in Christ. To receive the Spirit is to receive the living Christ, and the indwelling Spirit is the indwelling Christ. Paul makes this quite clear: "The Lord [meaning Christ] is the Spirit";[15] "The last Adam [meaning Christ] became a life-giving spirit." [16] In the new aeon of the Spirit old barriers of time and space crumble before the glorified Christ as he makes his life-changing impact, person to person, upon men of all ages and all lands and gives them access to the resources of his Spirit.

The true nature of Christian stewardship becomes clear only in the perspective of the new age of the Spirit. Paul's words, "Any one who does not have the spirit of Christ does not belong to him," have a definite application here. No one can be a Christian steward until the Holy Spirit has led him into the presence of the living Christ and a genuine personal commitment to Christ has taken place. Conversely, such a commitment cannot but lead to that vital wholehearted consecration which is the essence of stewardship. The faith generated by the Holy Spirit, Lord and

[14] Acts 2:33-36.   [15] II Cor. 3:17.   [16] I Cor. 15:45.

Giver of life, is living faith. It is not mere adherence to regulations, laws, and codes, "for the written code kills, but the Spirit gives life." [17] It is not bound to rites and ceremonies, traditions and institutions, for "where the Spirit of the Lord is, there is freedom," [18] freedom from the tyranny of external forms. It is life in its joyful spontaneity and exuberant power. It is life consummated in the presence of God and in partnership with God. Its motto is "I live; yet not I, but Christ liveth in me." It does not know Christ "according to the flesh" as only a historical figure to be remembered, a teacher to be followed, a model to be copied. It knows Christ "according to the Spirit" as a divine presence with whom to walk, a friend to whom one may entrust oneself completely. Faith is realizing the fulfilment of the promise, "Lo, I am with you always." Faith is venturing forth with him in ever more courageous exploits for the attainment of the purposes which we share with him, assured that in the new age of his victorious lordship, through the power and guidance of his Spirit, ever "greater works than these" are possible.

THE COMMUNITY OF THE SPIRIT

The Holy Spirit and the holy Christian church are inseparable. Pentecost, the day on which the Lord fulfilled his promise of sending the Spirit, is also the day which the church celebrates as its birthday. The Spirit who created in the hearts of the first Christians a new life in Christ also united their hearts in a new community of love. "All who believed were together and had all things in common. . . . The company of those who believed were of one heart and soul." [19] It was through this community which he himself had created that the Spirit continued to bestow the blessings of the new age, new vital contact with Christ and the resulting new insight, new courage, and new strength. Through this community the glorified Christ was to manifest his

[17] II Cor. 3:6.   [18] II Cor. 3:17.   [19] Acts 2:44; 4:32.

68

saving sovereignty and to carry God's purpose for the world to its completion. The divine stewardship "plan for the fulness of time" [20] culminates in the Spirit-born and Spirit-empowered community which is to extend to the ends of the earth to bring the saving presence of the living Christ to men everywhere. The God who became incarnate in Jesus now makes his residence in the hearts of all believers through a continuing and growing incarnation in which the Lord who has become a life-giving Spirit reveals his full stature. "He [God] has put all things under his feet . . . *for the church*, which is his body, the fulness of him who fills all in all." [21]

The rediscovery of this profound New Testament conception of the nature of the church, its organic relation to Christ and to the Holy Spirit and its important role in the plan of God, is the most significant insight of the theology of the twentieth century. It has given new depth, vitality, and incentive to the ecumenical movement, the effort of Christians of varying backgrounds to find their oneness in Christ. It is of equal importance to the stewardship movement, the effort of Christians to realize in life and deed the meaning of church membership. In chapter II we have already noted the inseparable connection between the Word of God and the people of God, and in chapter VII we shall give specific attention to the church as the covenant people of God. The task now is to point out the stewardship implications of the New Testament teaching that the church is the community of the Holy Spirit.

The superficiality of much of the popular thinking on stewardship is due in a large measure to superficial views on the nature of the church and of church membership. To a child the church is a building to which people go to learn about God. To his parents, who are members of the congregation which worships there, the church is that congregation. Since it teaches people

[20] Eph. 1:9. [21] Eph. 1:22.

how to live right, it is a valuable asset to the community. All good people ought to "join" it, regardless of how many other organizations they have already joined, and support it as well as they can. But having joined, they discover that the local congregation is a unit in a larger organization, nation-wide in its scope, and the conception of stewardship must be broadened to include "the whole work of the whole church." In many other lands than ours the ideas of joining and supporting have no relevance, for the church is to ordinary people an imposing national institution, like the state, supported by taxation and baptizing everyone into its membership quite automatically. Finally, in recent years, many have heard about an emerging great church and have come to believe that the ideal church is a world organization of Christians of all lands and all denominations.

To the gospel and the theology based upon it all this talk of joining and supporting, of organization and institution, is entirely beside the point in defining the essence of the church. It is a highly debatable question whether our Lord founded a church at all in the popular connotation of that word. He did gather a group of followers about him and gave the promise, "where two or three are gathered in my name, there am I in the midst of them." [22] In one oft-debated passage he said, "On this rock I will build my church," [23] but even here the emphasis is on the confession of faith, "You are the Christ, the Son of the living God," to which he was responding, and there is no indication that he had the founding of an ecclesiastical institution in mind. To the apostolic church likewise organizational and institutional considerations were altogether secondary. The structure of the community formed on Pentecost was simple indeed: "those who received his word were baptized . . . and they devoted themselves to the apostles' teaching and fellowship, to the breaking of bread

[22] Matt. 18:20.   [23] Matt. 16:18.

and the prayers." [24] Even several decades later when the Epistle to the Ephesians first gave articulate expression to the thought that the scattered groups of Christians then dotting the Roman Empire constituted one universal church, the sole constitutive and unifying factor was held to be the Spirit. The emphasis is on maintaining "the unity of the Spirit in the bond of peace," for there is "one Lord, one faith, one baptism, one God and Father." [25] To be sure, the rudiments of institutional procedure are discernible from the outset because of the necessity of preventing disorder. The manifestations of the Spirit tended to be accompanied by such outbursts of emotional frenzy that Paul had to lay down regulations for channeling the enthusiasm into constructive use and to demand that "all things should be done decently and in order." [26] Nor could the church be indifferent to the questions of how and by whom its sacred ordinances were administered, its message proclaimed, and its mission carried out. But it is important to bear in mind that the emergence of definite ecclesiastical forms of organization and the crystallization of specific ways of work and worship belong to history and tradition, not to the gospel itself. A church true to the gospel cannot define itself as anything else than the community of those whom the Holy Spirit has united with Christ. Nothing else is of constitutive importance.

When through the course of the centuries the church had undergone a transformation from a community of the Spirit into an ecclesiastical institution, it is no mere coincidence that the rediscovery of the gospel led also to the rediscovery of the true nature of the church. "The essence, life, and nature of Christendom," declares Luther, "is not a bodily assembly but an assembly of hearts in one faith. . . . It is a spiritual unity, on account of which men are called the communion of saints. And this unity is of itself enough to constitute Christendom, and without it no

[24] Acts 2:41-42.   [25] Eph. 4:3-6.   [26] I Cor. 14:40.

unity, be it of place, of time, of person, of work, or of whatever else, makes Christendom. . . . Christendom is different from all temporal communities, since it is nothing external. . . . The real, true, essential Christendom is a spiritual thing, and not anything external or outward. . . . For a person who is not a Christian may have all those other things, but they will never make him a Christian if he does not have faith, which alone makes Christians." [27] The Reformer recognized, of course, the proper place of external things in the work of the church. The mission for which the Spirit uses the fellowship implies proclaimers and hearers, time and place and equipment, all the manifold means and structures of organized activity. But the institution is the instrument of the Word, not the Word the instrument of the institution. In proclaiming the Word through which the Holy Spirit generates faith, the church becomes "the mother that bears every Christian through the Word." [28] In keeping with these fundamental insights of the Reformation the Augsburg Confession defines the church as "the congregation of saints (or assembly of believers) in which the Gospel is rightly taught and the Sacraments rightly administered."

The limits of our task permit reference to only a few of the rich contributions which the theology of the present century has made toward understanding the nature of the church. The pioneer among the Swedish theologians who have done much to rediscover the primitive concept of the church and to revitalize the heritage of the Reformation was Bishop Einar Billing, who stressed the fundamental principle that the church is God's own activity, what he does through the Word and the sacraments, not the activity of men who have decided to organize. Since the heart of this activity is the forgiveness of sins, the essence of the church is the divine grace of forgiveness, freely offered to all and leading

[27] *W.A.* 6, 292 ff.
[28] *Large Catechism*, II, 42.

those who accept it in an exodus from bondage to a new life of willing service. Closely related is Bishop Nygren's emphasis that the key to the nature of the church is the nature of Christ and to be "in Christ" is to be a living member of his body, the church.

The same thought is presented by Karl Heim in a still sharper form: "the members of the church are not adherents or pupils or disciples of Christ but ingredients of the expanded personality of Christ himself." [29] Christ alone has unbroken fellowship with God, and if our fellowship with God is real, it means that we have entered into Christ and become constitutive parts of his person. The church is the continuing presence and activity of the glorified Christ in history. To Oscar Cullmann the church is the visible center of the kingdom of Christ. The ascended Christ is the Lord of all life, the ruler over all principalities and powers, but the members of his church are those subjects who are aware of his sovereignty and consciously loyal to him. The latest noteworthy contribution is made by Emil Brunner who defines the church as "the oneness of communion with Christ by faith and brotherhood in love." [30] Brunner warns against the identification of the church with any institutional structure, which can be at best only its destructible external vessel, and stresses the abiding nature of the church as a community created and sustained by the Holy Spirit.

These theological insights into the divine origin, nature, and function of the church must become the property of ordinary Christian believers if the practical activities of Christian stewardship are to serve their true purpose. Otherwise a dangerous cleavage is introduced between what the church is by definition and what it is in its actual life and work. It is not enough for theologians to point out that the externals with which the existing ecclesiastical institutions are concerned do not belong to the

[29] *Jesus der Weltvollender*, Berlin, 1937, p. 246.
[30] *Das Missverständnis der Kirche*, Stuttgart, 1951, p. 107.

essence of the church. If the church is the community and agency of the Holy Spirit, it means that the external things it works with do not remain mere externals but take on a sacramental quality as instruments of the Spirit. If the church is the continuing incarnation of Christ, it means that the Word which it accepts in faith continues to become flesh in its life, that the features of Christ become ever more discernible in all that it says and does. Just as Jesus could say, "Who has seen me has seen the Father," so the aim of the church must be to be able to say, "Who has seen me has seen Christ." And if the church is the visible aspect of the kingdom, then its light must so shine before men that they may see its good works and give glory to God.

The stewardship implications growing out of the nature of the church may perhaps be most concisely stated by examining some of the principal words and images which the early church used in describing itself. The root of the word "church" itself, the Greek adjective *kyriakos* (belonging to the Lord), is used in the New Testament to modify the Lord's Supper[31] and the Lord's day.[32] Thus the very word *church* carries the fundamental stewardship idea of divine ownership. The church is Christ's church, not ours, just as he is the host at the Lord's table, not we. The church exists not for our enjoyment but for the doing of his work, the achievement of his purposes.

The basic New Testament noun for the word church is *ekklesia*, meaning literally a body of people who have been "called out." In classical Greek it referred to a political assembly of the citizens of a city state, summoned and convened by a herald. In the Septuagint, the Greek translation of the Old Testament, it was used to translate *qahal*, the assembly of Israel, the people whom God called from among the nations to be his own covenant people. Fundamental to the concept of the church is recognition of the fact that it is not a mere association of like-

[31] I Cor. 11:20.   [32] Rev. 1:10.

minded people organized to advance a purpose they have in common but a community that comes into being by divine appointment. The church has its origin in the will of God. Its members are men whom God has chosen and called, who have responded to his call, entered into his covenant, accepted a holy commission as stewards of his eternal purpose.

One of the simplest and yet most meaningful of the many images with which the New Testament portrays the church is that of "the flock." Applying to himself the Old Testament picture of God and his Messiah as shepherd-king,[33] our Lord describes himself as the Good Shepherd who lays down his life for the sheep and has other sheep besides the ancient covenant people, all of whom he seeks to gather into one fold.[34] "Fear not, little flock," he assures his followers, "for it is your Father's good pleasure to give you the kingdom." [35] The apostles likewise speak of the church as "the flock of God," of which Christ is the Chief Shepherd and for which he has shed his blood.[36] Here, says Luther, is a definition of the church which even a child seven years old can understand: "lambs who hear the voice of their shepherd." [37] This metaphor has its own important contribution to make to the concept of stewardship. "My sheep heed my voice," says the Good Shepherd. To be a member of his flock is to be sensitive to His Word, to yield him simple trustful obedience, to "follow the Lamb wherever he goes." [38]

Another significant metaphor is contained in our Lord's words: "I am the vine, you are the branches." [39] This figure too represents an old biblical tradition, that of calling the people of God his vineyard or his field. In using it to describe the unique and intimate relation between himself and his people, Jesus gives it

---

[33] E.g., Isa. 40:11; Ezek. 34:23; Ps. 23.
[34] John 10:11-18. [35] Luke 12:32. [36] Acts 20:38; I Pet. 5:2.
[37] "The Church" in *Smalcald Articles.*
[38] Rev. 14:4. [39] John 15:5.

new depth and vitality. Just as the vine and the branches constitute one inseparable and living whole, so Jesus relates to himself the entire life of the church. The church is not formed by an association of individuals who have come together any more than the vine is formed by putting together various separate branches. It is the outgrowth and activity of Jesus' own life. To be in the church, in the true sense, is to be "in Christ." Of particular significance to stewardship is the practical application which our Lord proceeds to make of this truth: "He who abides in me, and I in him, he it is that bears much fruit. . . . If a man does not abide in me, he is cast forth as a branch and withers; and the branches are gathered, thrown into the fire and burned." [40] The church as an external organization may have dead branches but the true vine does not. Insofar as the church is truly the church its members bear fruit in a life of stewardship.

Similar vital insights may be derived from the figures of speech with which Paul describes the nature of the church. Even when the apostle uses such a static figure as that of a building,[41] he cannot avoid introducing the idea of life and growth in the realization of God's purpose. In the living Christ "the whole structure is joined together and grows into a holy temple in the Lord." [42] The members of the church are constantly being "built into it for a dwelling place of God in the Spirit," [43] a thought echoed in I Peter, where they are called "living stones." [44] They are also described as "fellow citizens with the saints" of a heavenly commonwealth, sharing its privileges and its responsibilities.[45] The warmth of home glows from the picture of the church as "the household of God" in which the obligations of stewardship are a family affair.[46]

The "great mystery" of the church as the beloved "bride

---

[40] John 15:5-6. [41] Eph. 2:20-22; I Cor. 3:9 ff. [42] Eph. 2:21.
[43] Eph. 2:22. [44] I Pet. 2:5. [45] Eph. 2:19; Phil. 3:20. [46] Eph. 2:19.

of Christ" points both to the profound unity between Christ and his church ("the two shall become one"), and to the obedience of love which this unity inspires. The true force of this beautiful metaphor is lost when it is detached from its context and interpreted only in emotional and mystical terms. The apostle's main emphasis is this: "As the church is subject to Christ, so let wives also be subject in everything to their husbands." [47] This submission in both cases is a submission called forth by love. "Husbands, love your wives, as Christ loved the church and gave himself up for her." [48] Such love is a purifying, transforming, sanctifying force: "that he might consecrate her, having cleansed her . . . that the church might be presented before him . . . without spot or wrinkle . . . that she might be holy and without blemish." [49] No forced exegesis is required to see here the ideal of a church inspired by the deepest motive and dedicated to the highest objective of Christian stewardship.

The strongest and most frequently used of Paul's metaphors of the church is that of the "body of Christ." This is the basis of the theological view that the church is the continuing incarnation, Christ himself active within the forms of historical existence, and thus a constitutive part of the glorified Christ. There can be no doubt that the apostle conceives of the church as no chance aggregation but a living organism united by the Holy Spirit to Christ, the Head. Through baptism we are incorporated into this organism, and through the Word and the Lord's Supper we are nourished and sustained in it. Since the teaching of the Word and the administration of the sacraments are visible activities of the organized church, the church can never remain a purely spiritual invisible entity. While that which the Spirit creates, both faith and "the assembly of hearts in faith," is spiritual in nature, its vitality becomes manifest in visible action. The church is the body of Christ, not an incorporeal idea. We can speak

[47] Eph. 5:24. [48] Eph. 5:25. [49] Eph. 5:27.

about an invisible church only with reference to the saints in heaven. In this world God works through incarnation. He became incarnate in the man Jesus, but the incarnation continues in the new age which began when the earthly mission of Jesus was accomplished. The Lord who is now the life-giving Spirit becomes incarnate in the church, as the faith and the fellowship which he creates assume visible form. Yet we cannot identify any one of the organized churches, or all of them taken together, with the incarnate Christ. Christ is not incarnate in those who are not "in Christ" although they have been baptized and have their names in the church register. Simon the magician was baptized and regarded as a "believer," yet Peter said to him, "You have neither part nor lot in this matter." [50] It would be blasphemous to regard the hosts of nominal or lukewarm members of the existing churches as members of the body of Christ.

The relation between the church as the living body of Christ and the church as an external organization with many lifeless members remains a hopeless paradox so long as we operate with static definitions. If the church is by definition the continuing incarnation of Christ and this incarnation inevitably assumes the form of institutional structure and procedure, then the institution appears to have the right to regard itself, as the Roman Catholic church does, as the body of Christ regardless of its obvious weaknesses and imperfections in comparison with the original incarnation. And if baptism is by definition incorporation into Christ, then all the baptized members of the organized church are members of the body of Christ whether they are true believers or not. The paradox is not solved by such distinctions as the church visible and invisible, the church in a broad sense and in a narrow sense, the church outward and inward. The only distinction of ultimate importance is the distinction between a living church and a dead church, a church that is what it is only by

[50] Acts 8:9-25.

definition and a church that lives up to its name. This is the distinction which the Lord of the church himself makes: "I know your works; you have the name of being alive, and you are dead." [51] Just as he judges the sincerity of calling him "Lord" by the obedience to which it leads, so he judges the genuineness of the church defining itself as the body of Christ by the measure in which it functions as the body of Christ. The living Christ refuses to identify himself with a dead body. The church can establish its identity with him only by his own method: "Abide in me and bear fruit."

Thus it is from the point of view of vital Christian stewardship that our paradox is solved and the metaphor of the body of Christ becomes more than a figure of speech. The organized church is the body of Christ when this profound term does not only define a theological concept but describes the actual life and work of the church. It is a constant summons to the church to realize its true nature and mission, to be what it defines itself to be. If Christ is in fact the Head and the church his body, then its thought and activity must be determined by him and he must be allowed to use its members as the head uses the members of the body. Then its life must be none other than Christ himself going forth to achieve his redeeming purpose. Its voice must be the voice of Christ proclaiming his eternal gospel. Its hands must be Christ's hands doing his works of love. Christ himself must look through our eyes, walk in our steps, love through our hearts. To describe the church as the body of Christ is to describe the church as living out the meaning of Christian stewardship.

We have traced stewardship to its source in the work of the Holy Spirit and the nature of the church. The theology which we have outlined is no innovation. It is the theology of the gospel and of the Reformation. We may appropriately close this section of our study with the following statements from one of the basic

[51] Rev. 3:1.

79

confessional formulations of this theology, the Apology of the Augsburg Confession. "In defining the church, it must unconditionally be defined as the *living* body of Christ." "Christ's kingdom is only that which he enlivens with his Spirit." "Those, therefore, in whom Christ does not effect anything are not members of Christ."

CHAPTER VI

Justification By Faith

We have observed that the new life which finds expression in
Christian stewardship is the work of the Holy Spirit, who confronts men with the living Christ and unites them with the body
of Christ, the church. We have also learned from the beginning
of our study that the Word which the Spirit speaks through the
church is an invitation to an encounter with the God incarnate
in Christ. We must now examine this encounter between God
and man. The issues before us are man and his sin, the application of the redemption secured by Christ to individual lives, the
achievement of the central purpose of the gospel to take man's
hand and place it in God's hand, the discovery of the ground
on which sinful men can enter into the partnership with God
implied by stewardship. These issues may be summed up in
the distressed question of the Philippian jailer: "What must I
do to be saved?" [1] The answer, "Believe in the Lord Jesus, and
you will be saved," receives its theological formulation in the
so-called "material principle" of evangelical theology, justification by faith. The pivotal importance of this doctrine is derived
from the fact that it contains the whole content of the gospel in
epitome. It describes the establishment of a personal fellowship
between man and God on the realistic basis that man is man, with
no illusions about himself, and God is God in all the sovereignty
of his holiness and love.

To introduce an analysis of the meaning of this doctrine for
the actual life of stewardship we may begin with a concrete
experience in which the gospel achieves its purpose. Our starting

[1] Acts 16:30.

point could be the encounter with God experienced by Paul[2] or Augustine or Wesley or Bunyan or many another. I have selected Luther because in his case the universally valid doctrinal implications stand out in such bold relief and have had such decisive influence in the shaping of modern evangelical theology.

Let us go back to the year 1505. Luther is twenty-two years old. He has two university degrees and is studying law. But now his inner struggles to find a confident personal relation to God are heightened by repeated contacts with death. Finally, as he is returning to his university at Erfurt, he is caught in an electric storm. A thunderbolt strikes dangerously close to him and he falls to the ground. The experience itself is nothing unique, any more than Newton's being struck by an apple. But just as Newton's experience is said to have been the occasion for the discovery of a basic law of physics, so the young Saxon is led by his experience to grasp the point of view of responsibility in the perspective of eternity. He sees how foolish it is to say, "I am the master of my fate," for in the hour of death another master calls and each individual "you" must answer. And if in the hour of death you must accept another master, is it not the highest wisdom to learn to know him and to accept him as master in every hour of life? Furthermore, you must answer his call *alone.* Even if you have nothing else on your own, if you have succeeded in shifting your responsibility upon others all your life, it will not work in the hour of death. You must do your own dying. Can anything, then, be more important than to learn to accept this personal responsibility in the light of eternity?

The gifted young man with a sensitive conscience gives up his career and enters a monastery to work out the solution to this problem. Now begin long years of bitter soul-struggles as he explores everything that the church has to offer to one who

---

[2] In *Resurgence of the Gospel,* pp. 42-47, I have presented an analysis of the experience which underlies the original formulation of this doctrine by Paul.

seeks honestly to bridge the gulf between God and man. Others are satisfied with second-bests such as "Do the best you can, and the church will take care of you." Not so Luther. He seeks what God himself has to say. He has been taught that a man can do what he genuinely wills to do but he discovers that the human will can meet only human requirements. God demands that man love him with all his heart, all his soul, all his strength, all his mind. Luther, like Paul before him, finds that he cannot do that. He has to discipline himself to love God, and forced love is not true love. In fact, as he looks still more deeply into his own heart, he finds that man seeks his own good even in God. He does not love God for the sake of God but for the sake of his own peace of mind and happiness. Thus Luther locates the main source for man's separation from God in man's incurable self-centeredness, which he calls original or personal sin. Man not only commits this or that act of sin but he is a sinner who cannot but love himself above all. His relation to the true God remains wrong, for even his religion is at bottom an idolatry of self. He does not let God be God but uses God to gain his own ends. The Reformation doctrines of sin and grace are not the result of armchair philosophizing; they are wrung from the depths of an agonized heart.

Finally the light of the gospel breaks through. Luther has become a professor at the University of Wittenberg and is preparing lectures on the Psalms. He comes to Psalm 71:2,[3] "Deliver me in thy righteousness." This strange prayer arrests him. How can sinful man appeal to God's righteousness for deliverance? Does not God's righteousness demand the punishment of the sinner instead of his rescue? He searches the Scriptures for an answer. He finds it in Romans 1:17: "For therein is the righteous-

[3] E. G. Schwiebert, following Vogelsang, points out that a fundamental change in Luther's interpretation of the Psalms does not become apparent until this point, not at Ps. 31:1 where the same prayer occurs. See Schwiebert, *Luther and His Times* (St. Louis: Concordia, 1950), pp. 287-289.

ness of God revealed from faith to faith: as it is written, the just shall live by faith." God's righteousness, then, is not the righteousness of the law courts. It is a redeeming righteousness. Fellowship between God and man is not established on God's level, for man can never climb there, but on man's level to which God descends. Salvation is not an achievement but a gift which God places in the open palm of faith. And the right response to a gift is not desperate struggle but joyful gratitude. To be made righteous is to be made *rightwise* with God, and this right relation is not based on what I can do or what has taken place in me but on what God in Christ has done for me. If we then confess our sins, God is righteous to forgive. God saves sinners, not in spite of his righteousness, but because of his righteousness. His justice is of a higher order than ours. It is a saving justice which justifies the unjust and can therefore be nothing else than his love for sinners. "Note this fact carefully," Luther proceeds to preach, "that when you find in the Scriptures the word God's justice . . . it means the revealed grace and mercy of God through Jesus Christ." [4] The light of the gospel, long hidden under the bushel of man-centered religiosity, shines forth once more. The frightened monk emerges from his cell a completely transformed man, a man with a message and a mission. He is a steward of the gospel, for he has discovered the meaning of the gospel.

To be an evangelical Christian is to make the same discovery for oneself. The form of the experience will vary with individuals, for God deals with us as persons, and no two persons are alike. Whether our experience of the gospel has an emotional or an educational pattern, whether it is abrupt or gradual, early in life or late, depends on the personality and the background of each individual. The analysis of the resulting varieties of experience is a matter for psychology, not theology. Insofar as these

[4] Sermon on the Gospel of the First Sunday in Advent, *Works*, Lenker edition, X, sec. 37.

experiences represent a genuine response to the Holy Spirit who through the gospel gives men a new relation to God and new life in Christ, the theological content is always the same. It is this: God justifies, that is, accepts with favor, the sinner who admits his own utter inability to be anything but a sinner and gratefully accepts fellowship with God as an entirely undeserved gift. Paul, the first great theologian of the gospel, expressed this theology of God's amazing friendship for sinners in such majestic assertions as these: "Since all have sinned and fall short of the glory of God, they are justified by his grace as a gift, through the redemption which is in Christ Jesus, whom God put forward as an expiation by his blood, to be received in faith," [5] and "Therefore being justified by faith, we have peace with God through our Lord Jesus Christ, by whom also we have access by faith into this grace wherein we stand: and rejoice in hope of the glory of God." [6] Here is the heart of the gospel, and the theology of the Reformation echoes clearly and strongly its throbs: *solus Christus*, Christ alone; *sola gratia*, by grace alone; *sola fide*, by faith alone. Or expressing these basic emphases more accurately in their interrelationship: man's fellowship with God is *propter Christum*, on account of Christ; *sola gratia*, by grace alone; *per fidem*, through faith.

Let us examine this theology a bit more closely. It is not necessary to discuss *solus Christus* at length in this connection, for the radical Christ-centeredness of all truly Christian stewardship has been the theme of our entire study. Let us simply observe that the Christ of the gospel of justification by faith is not merely a historical figure whose teachings we are asked to accept and whose example we are asked to follow. He is infinitely more than teacher or prophet, lawgiver or model. He is Mediator and Savior. He is *Christus pro nobis*, the Christ who offered himself as sacrifice *for us*. He is the Son of Man who came "to seek

[5] Rom. 3:23-25.   [6] Rom. 5:1-2.

85

that which is lost," "to give his life as a ransom for many." He is the Lamb of God whose blood was "poured out for many for the forgiveness of sins." He is the Lord who claimed the divine prerogative of forgiving sins and commissioned his apostles to preach "repentance and forgiveness of sins in his name to all nations."

These profound assertions by Christ himself are the basic roots of the doctrine of justification by faith. When, on this basis, Paul reflects on the drama of the Cross in the light of his own encounter with the living and pardoning Christ, the doctrine assumes its form: "God shows his love for us in that while we were yet sinners Christ died for us . . . we are now justified by his blood . . . [he was] raised for our justification." When the full significance of this doctrine is grasped as it was by the Reformers, it means nothing less than a Copernican revolution in religion. Man's quest for God gives way to God's quest for man. The axiom of all natural religiosity, "Man must do something to make God his friend," is now inverted, "God does everything in his power to make man his friend." Instead of saying, "Goodness is necessary for salvation" we must now say, "Salvation is necessary for goodness." Our godliness has nothing to do with our finding favor with God, for God justifies the ungodly on the basis of what Christ has done for sinners.

Sola gratia, by grace alone, focuses attention upon the unique character of this divine saving activity. Here lies the peculiarity of the gospel, the trait that distinguishes it from all other forms of religion. Man is not asked to do anything, to achieve anything, to meet any requirements. Here is instead an insight into the heart of God and this remarkable discovery: God has it in his heart to love sinners *as they are.* Let us recall once more the picture of God given in the story of the prodigal son. The father cannot wait until the boy has come to the door but runs down the road to meet him. And the boy has no chance to speak the words of repentance which he has rehearsed at the swine-trough before the father's lips are upon his and the father's arms embrace him. Here is sheer redemptiveness that recognizes no rational or moral restrictions. Or think of the thief on the cross, whose life from the moral point of view had been such a disgraceful failure that, by his own acknowledgment, he deserved nothing but capital punishment. Yet his plea "Remember me" brings the response "Today thou shalt be with me in paradise" without a word of judgment being spoken. The deep calls unto deep, the depth of distress to the depth of grace, and not in vain.

Grace may be described as God's most effective strategy in dealing with man's tragic predicament, the supreme demonstration that he is God and his ways are not our ways. To Paul it was God's new way of salvation which supplanted the old way, the effort to keep the law. What a terrific inner struggle this Pharisee of the Pharisees must have gone through before he could confess: the law is not the way of salvation, the grace of our Lord Jesus Christ is, and Christ is the end of the law. The new strategy is that of sovereign love which is not conditioned by its object, which draws no line between the worthy and the unworthy, which does not seek but creates the lovable object. In Luther's words, "Sinners are not loved because they are lovely, they are lovely because they are loved." [7] God is God, the Giver of every good and perfect gift, including the gift of eternal life. He alone is righteous but it is the glory of his grace to ascribe his own righteousness to guilty sinners. They are justified, not on the basis of what they have done or will do, but solely on the basis of what Christ has done for them. Justification by the law would be an acquittal of the innocent. Justification by grace is an acquittal of the guilty. We are and remain sinners who deserve only judgment, but grace is undeserved love to which no

W.A. 1, 365, 11.

conditions are attached. It is freely given and asks only to be freely received.

Sola fide, by faith alone, the third emphasis in justification, calls attention to the only role which man plays in justification, namely, that of receiving God's grace. The expression "justification by faith" is actually misleading, for faith is neither the ground nor the cause of justification. The ground is the redemptive work of Christ and the cause is grace, God's love for sinners. Faith is our acceptance of what God in Christ has done for us and offers to us. It is commitment into the hands of the God revealed in Christ. It is a basic life-orientation, just as sin is. "Whatever does not proceed from faith is sin," says Paul. Faith is the God-centered attitude, just as sin is the self-centered attitude. Its first trait is receptivity. This is the spiritual poverty, concern, hunger and thirst, childlikeness, which Jesus makes the one entrance requirement into the kingdom and which opened the door into paradise to the thief on the cross. "Where meek souls will receive him still, the dear Christ enters in." The second trait is trust. Faith is to entrust oneself to Christ as a patient about to undergo an operation entrusts himself to the surgeon. It is to allow him to take full charge, to stop struggling on our own, swinging between pride and despair. And the third trait is obedience. It is not merely accepting something as true. It is accepting a new Lord and a new life in responsibility.

Justification as such is a purely objective divine act which has no reference to any change within us, either as its condition or its consequence. It refers only to our altered relation to God. We are now pardoned sinners but still sinners. We are pronounced righteous but not made righteous, for we continue to depend on the grace of forgiveness. But faith, our subjective response to this grace, signifies the entrance of a new life-changing power, the beginning of a lifelong struggle between the old man and the new. The change from pride, self-interest, and acquisitiveness to the dependence, confidence, and obedience of faith involves such a thoroughgoing reconstruction of natural life that it can be described only as a new birth. It may be portrayed as repentance, change of mind, or conversion, change of direction, but best of all as regeneration, the gift of a new life. As such it is entirely the work of the Holy Spirit. He begets us again by the Word of truth. He enables us to make the basic affirmation of faith, "Jesus is my Lord." He testifies with our spirit that we are the children of God. He unites us with the living Christ and with his people.

The most important thing about faith is neither its quality nor its quantity but its object. It is saying with Paul, "I know *in whom* I have believed." Faith is a personal relationship. It cannot be weighed or measured. When the disciples came to Jesus with the plea, "Lord, increase our faith," he at once directed their attention away from such computation and said, "If you had faith as a grain of mustard seed, you could say to this sycamine tree, 'be rooted up, and be planted in the sea,' and it would obey you." [8] Faith, the Lord implies, is our connection with God, and its power is not in the connection but in the God with whom we are connected. If we are united with his illimitable resources, then things which to us are impossible become possible. Faith is thus an all-or-none proposition. As St. Augustine puts it, faith is *haerere Deo*, a clinging to God, but either you cling with all your might or you do not cling at all. Too often what passes for faith is the self-centered old Adam in new clothes. It is faith in our own faith, a nervous fingering of the pulse of our own religiousness. The only concern of true faith is through the Word and prayer to keep the channel open for the inflow of God's power and through obedient love to be the channel for the outflow of that power into the lives of others.

What bearing does this gospel of Christ, grace, and faith have

[8] Luke 17:6.

upon stewardship? There can be only one answer: this gospel is the heart and soul of Christian stewardship. Let me try to indicate how this basic theology answers three vital questions regarding stewardship: first, its beginning; second, its motivation; third, its method.

Let us consider first, then, the beginning of the life of stewardship. The doctrine of justification by grace presupposes that man is a sinner, a rebel against God's rule. Our stewardship cannot be traced to the divine sonship we have on the basis of creation, for we have lost that sonship and both the willingness and the power to carry out the tasks which it implies. The gospel does not make its appeal to man's innate goodness, his sense of duty, the altruistic impulses in his nature. It is the good news that God himself has engaged in triumphant redeeming action to overcome man's sin and in his sovereign grace establishes fellowship with man on the basis of forgiveness. Nor can the beginning of stewardship be traced directly to the objective act of justification itself. When deliverance from sin is by grace alone, it is God's own act which neither needs nor permits any human co-operation. Justification is not what God does *with* sinners but what he does *for* sinners. It is the utterly unique, sovereign, and paradoxical act of God who triumphs over sin by giving himself as sacrifice, who sets us free from the guilt of sin by making his Son to be sin. But this divine strategy achieves its end only when the objective redemptive act is personally appropriated in the commitment of faith. It is faith, the wholehearted grateful response to God's redeeming love, that is the true beginning of Christian stewardship. Stewardship is faith in action. In Dr. Stoughton's simple words, "It is what I do after I have said, 'I believe.'" The term "stewardship" is of course often used in a wider connotation. Every moral judgment, in fact, is a summons to act. When I have acknowledged anything to be good, it becomes my duty to do something about it. But

Christian stewardship concerns only Christian believers, those who through faith have received the gift of new life in Christ. "Without faith," says the writer of Hebrews, "it is impossible to please him [God]." [9] A stewardship that does not originate in the response of faith to the grace of God is not Christian stewardship. In the gospel by which the church lives the *Gabe* always precedes the *Aufgabe*. The gift comes first and only after that comes the task.

This truth is given vivid expression in the opening verses of the Second Epistle of Peter. The apostolic writer speaks first of the precious faith which has been given to us through the righteousness of God and our Savior Jesus Christ, of the grace and peace that are multiplied to us, of the divine power that has given to us all things that pertain to life and godliness, of the exceeding great and precious promises by which we have become partakers of God's own nature. Only after that he asks us to make every effort to express our faith in terms of virtue, knowledge, self-control, steadfastness, godliness, and love. "These things," he concludes, "keep you from being ineffective or unfruitful in the knowledge of our Lord Jesus Christ." The first question to be settled was: "Be of good cheer, thy sins are forgiven thee." After that it was: "Go and sin no more." So deep, in fact, are the roots of this sequence that they extend all the way back to the first of the Ten Commandments. It is the Lord who has brought his people out of the land of Egypt, delivered them from the house of bondage, who asks for their singlehearted loyalty: "Thou shalt have no other gods before me." Their life of obedience is grounded in his act of deliverance.

The problem of the relation between God's activity and man's activity is one which theologians have debated through the centuries. The Bible clearly ascribes all good works to God's activity in man and yet repeatedly exhorts us to do good works. Paul

[9] Heb. 11:6.

91

brings the two emphases together in one apparently paradoxical statement: "Work out your own salvation with fear and trembling; for God is at work in you, both to will and to work for his good pleasure." [10] You must work with utmost conscientiousness because God does it all! Moralists from Pelagius on have overstressed the truth contained in the first half of the statement, "Work out your own salvation," often to the point of virtually ignoring the divine factor. Monergistic theologians from Augustine on have tended to emphasize the second half so strongly that little room has been left for human responsibility. A mediating position is represented by the synergists, who attempt to solve the dilemma in terms of divine-human co-operation in which the activity and the responsibility are ascribed partly to God and partly to man. While this position lacks theological depth, it seems to supply more incentive to action than the dialectical theology which simply retains the paradox: Man must do something, although God has already done everything to be done.

Paul himself offers the solution to the paradox. He does not say, "Man must act *although* God acts," but "*because* God acts." The indicative of God's action is the basis for the imperative of man's action. Ethelbert Stauffer has produced conclusive evidence to show that this is the teaching of the New Testament as a whole. He sums up the solution in the following pointed sentences: "God's active will summons man's will to action. . . . God's action becomes effective in man's. God himself is at work in our work. The grace of God is potential energy which seeks actualization. The Spirit is at one and the same time a gift and a task. Divine election means being called to serve. . . . As the power of God's will grows the effort of man's will does not decrease, but grows." [11] This is a theological way of saying that the redeeming will of God to which we owe our salvation realizes

[10] Phil. 2:12-13.
[11] Ethelbert Stauffer, *New Testament Theology* (New York: Macmillan, 1955), pp. 181-184, 305.

92

itself in vital and growing Christian stewardship of life.

The gospel of justifying grace gives stewardship not only its starting point but also, in the second place, the power which motivates it and keeps it going. In the third chapter of *Ephesians* Paul describes the great things that Christ can do in our lives, the joy, the strength, the peace, the steadiness which result from faith in him. All this, he says, happens "by the action of his power within us." [12] The word which he uses is his favorite word for the gospel, *dynamis*, power. We who are standing on the threshold of the atomic age and learning to think of the release of energies that stagger the imagination are in position to appreciate what the discovery of the gospel meant to Paul. He had come upon resources more tremendous and revolutionary than he had ever imagined, a power that was able to do exceeding abundantly above all that we ask or think. That is precisely the way our Lord wanted his gospel to be understood. He never spoke of religion at all. To have faith meant to him to have life and to have it in abundance, in its divine fulness and strength. If you have faith, he said, you can remove mountains, and nothing shall be impossible to you. This is because faith is access to God's own boundless sources of power.

Here is indeed the secret of our strength. From the point of view of life in Christ we are wrong in supposing that in each of us is a reservoir containing a limited amount of energy. Under this false conception we try to economize our little store of strength lest we use it up too soon. A Christian is a channel, not a reservoir; a conductor, not a receptacle. Our strength does not come from our tugging and straining. It does not depend on our hoarding what little we have but on our making the right adjustment to God so that his power can flow through us.

Anyone who has engaged in the practical stewardship work of the church can appreciate the vital importance of this teaching.

[12] Eph. 3:20, Moffatt.

I have heard a representative of a professional fund-raising agency make the remark, "I have observed that the more often church people are asked to make substantial contributions, the better are the chances of success." This should be the normal situation, for once the hoarding attitude is overcome there is increased joy in increased giving. On the other hand, can anything be more discouraging than the effort to persuade people who are only nominally Christians to contribute to the work of the church according to the measure of their prosperity? Enthusiasms drawn from natural human resources are soon used up, and the exhortation to give more and more becomes wearisome both to the exhorter and the exhorted. Too often the final resort is to a legalistic "You must." "You must try harder."

To flog people to try harder to do better is, of course, a complete perversion of the gospel. To admonish man who is by nature self-centered to love God with his whole heart and to show that love in appropriate giving is truly to try to gather grapes from thorns and figs from thistles. One who is not in love cannot love. The attempt to force love is as cruel as it is futile. It is like telling a soldier whose legs have been shot off to get up and march. First make the tree good, says our Lord, and only then have you the right to expect good fruit. It is of the essence of the gospel that it is an "engrafted word" containing the gift of a new life which changes the human heart from within. To use Luther's fine phrase, it enables us to serve God "hilari et libera voluntate," with a hilarious and free will. Instead of groaning under the burden of coercive obligations, we rise with Christ into the joy, the peace, and the strength of the new aeon. We share in the blessing: "May the God of peace who brought again from the dead our Lord Jesus, . . . equip you with everything good that you may do his will, working in you that which is pleasing in his sight." [13] The power by which Christian stew-

[13] Heb. 13:20-21.

ardship operates is the power which once broke through the rock-hewn tomb in Joseph's garden to conquer death, the power by which a new heaven and a new earth will be created.

The primary concern of our stewardship is to have connection with that power. Let us suppose, suggests Karl Heim, that the wheels of a large factory suddenly came to a stop. In vain the engineers inspect and oil the machinery. That is not where the trouble lies. The flow of power has been cut off, and without it even the most perfect machines are useless. So it is with the church. We may improve our methods and techniques and pour increased apportionments of budgetary oil into the machinery, but the most resplendent and financially well-lubricated ecclesiastical machines are worthless unless we are connected with him who says, "Without me you can do nothing."

What does the gospel of justification by grace have to offer, finally, to the question of the *method* of our stewardship? We have already been driven by inescapable logic to recognize the inadequacy of moral exhortation and high-pressure coercion. A man who is cold needs to be led to a fire, not to be exhorted to get warm. Just so the cold and greedy hearts of men need to experience the warmth of the Savior's love before there will be a genuine spontaneous commitment to him, ensuing in a devoted life partnership with him. To lead men into the stewardship life is to lead men to Christ. The cause of stewardship and the cause of evangelism are thus at bottom one and the same. The purpose of these activities is not adequately defined in terms of getting people to join the church and to shoulder the obligations of church membership. The true goal in both cases is a personal wholehearted decision for Christ. And the major strategy in achieving this goal can be none other than God's own strategy in winning back to himself a mankind that had become estranged from him. The Word becomes flesh and confronts men with such sincere and persistent love that it prefers to suffer all their meanness rather than to abandon them to their estrangement. When they know no better than to reward him with a horrible death on a cross, he accepts that rather than allow himself to become separated from them. All truly Christian service wears the form of the Suffering Servant, bears the pattern of the cross. The strategy of the cross is to surround men with so much constant and resourceful love that they must do themselves violence not to surrender to it. It refuses to become embittered or discouraged even in the face of apparent failure. It accepts no rebuff as final, for it knows that "Love never faileth." Whatever tactics we use, this major strategy must always be kept in mind. It gives stewardship the winsome and patient resourcefulness which is the keynote of the gospel.

In pointing out the proper beginning, motive, and method of Christian stewardship, the doctrine of justification by grace serves as a constant reminder of the true relation of faith and the works of love. We are saved, as Luther taught, *sola fide*, by faith alone, not, as Aquinas taught, *fide caritate formata*, by faith fashioned by love. It is faith that energizes love, not love that energizes faith. Faith lives by God's love, not our own. But faith which does not produce the works of love is not true faith. As our Lord teaches in his parable of the great assize, the basis of God's final judgment will be not the mere profession of faith but the quality of life resulting from the acceptance or rejection of his grace. True believers have shown the genuineness of their faith through self-forgetting deeds of love. These have not been performed for merit, hence no record has been kept of them. "Lord, when did we do these things?" But such a life attitude is a manifestation of living faith which transforms men from their natural self-centeredness into the likeness of the God of love. We may thus fittingly conclude our study of the stewardship implications of the central principle of evangelical theology with

Paul's words: "The grace of God has appeared for the salvation of all men, training us to renounce irreligion and worldly passions, and to live sober, upright, and godly lives in this world, awaiting our blessed hope, the appearing of the glory of our great God and Savior Jesus Christ, who gave himself for us to redeem us from all iniquity and to purify for himself a people of his own who are zealous for good deeds." [14]

[14] Titus 2:11-14.

CHAPTER VII

The Priesthood of All Believers

"We are all priests." [1] "As many of us as have been baptised are all priests without distinction." [2] This was one of the first trumpet blasts of the Reformation. But Luther did not invent this startling doctrine. He discovered it in the gospel. When the New Testament says, "You are a royal priesthood" [3] and "He made us . . . priests," [4] it is not speaking about ordination but about the priesthood of every Christian man and woman. To be a priest is to be consecrated to serve God and fellow-man, and this is the calling of every Christian.

This doctrine, more than any other in evangelical theology, has captured the interest of Christian laymen in our day, spurred them to such activities as stewardship and evangelism, and provided theological sanction for these activities. This is because it is a doctrine which gives laymen something to do. The other doctrines which we have studied all have important implications with regard to the basis, the content, and the motivation of stewardship. The priesthood of all believers supplies a specific program of action. What a revolution it would mean in our churches were the dynamic conception of church membership contained in this doctrine once more to prevail in all its original power. No more would people hold the utterly unevangelical idea that once they have united with a congregation they have done their duty when they attend church and carry their share of the budget with which a man is hired to keep the organization running. No longer could a Christian congregation be described as a "bourgeois ghetto," a closed corporation of nice, respectable,

[1] "Babylonian Captivity of the Church," *Works*, Holman edition, II, p. 283.
[2] *Ibid.*, p. 279.
[3] I Pet. 2:9. [4] Rev. 1:6.

middle-class people. No longer would the worship service on Sunday be an end in itself. It would be a means for releasing the resources of the gospel into the daily person-to-person contacts wherever "cross the crowded ways of life." The church would cease to be an institution chiefly concerned with maintaining its forms, traditions, and divisions. It would meet the world once more as a Spirit-empowered, united, and witnessing fellowship.

Universal spiritual priesthood derives its importance, first of all, from the fact that it makes a vital application of the doctrine of Christ and the doctrine of the church. It sets forth the basic truth that Jesus is the Messiah and the church is the people of the Messiah. When the apostolic community described itself as "a chosen race, a royal priesthood, a holy nation, God's own people," [5] it appropriated for itself the status of the covenant people of God in which the messianic hope had been fulfilled. Far from being merely an association of people with similar interests, it was the culmination of a divine plan, the instrument by which God carries out his redeeming strategy for mankind. As such it had a prenatal existence, so to speak, within the chosen people of the Old Covenant. Hence Paul characterizes it as "the Israel of God," "Abraham's offspring," "heirs according to promise," "the true circumcision." The Messiah had now come. His life, death, and resurrection had inaugurated the new age in which the promised New Covenant was to be realized. For those who are "in Christ" the messianic age had already begun. Through his resurrection Christ had won a decisive victory over the demonic powers of the evil old age and gave his people the assurance that every enemy is a defeated enemy. Through the gift of the Spirit they had a guarantee of ultimate victory and access to the resurrection power by which it was to be achieved. The church is the first fruits of the new age, the colony of heaven on earth, the stronghold established in enemy-held terri-

[5] I Pet. 2:9.

tory by the Messiah in his conquest to win back all creation for God.

Particularly important for stewardship is the New Testament teaching that every member of the messianic community shares in the Messiah's own mission. "As the Father has sent me," he tells his people, "even so I send you." [6] You have been constituted a "royal priesthood," wrote Peter, "that you may declare the wonderful deeds of him who called you out of darkness into his marvelous light." [7] A unique status and mission is thus given to Christian *laymen*. The very word is derived from *laos*, people, the word which the New Testament uses to designate the messianic people, the royal priesthood. To be a Christian layman, then, is to be a priest and a king, a Christ man and a kingdom man. The crucial question is whether a man is "in Christ," a living member of his body, the church, and sharing in the work of his kingdom, or whether he is on the outside. That distinction is far more important than the one between minister and layman. Another term which the New Testament uses to designate the kingdom people is "saints." It characterizes both their relation to their Lord, who has called them from the sinful life of the world and consecrates them to be his people, and their relation to the world, to which they are living "letters from Christ." He calls them out of the world into God's kingdom and then sends them back into the world to do the work of the kingdom. Christian saintliness is not a monastic withdrawal from the world for the sake of seeking sinlessness for oneself. It is self-forgetting service to others by the power of him who uses imperfect instruments to accomplish his holy purposes.

Underlying the conception of Christian believers as "priests" and "saints" is the doctrine of sanctification, the work of the Holy Spirit in energizing faith into holiness of life. The importance of this doctrine for Christian stewardship is obvious. In a

⁸ John 20:21. ⁷ I Pet. 2:9.

broad sense the whole theology of stewardship is a study of sanctification. It is a description of the process whereby God's will becomes implanted in ours. In sanctification the grace of forgiveness, the new life in Christ, and membership in the kingdom become the vital realities of consecrated stewardship, and conversely a faith that does not produce this result is dead faith.

But lest we mistake our own emotional experiences or moral successes for the achievement of perfection, the dependence of sanctification upon justification must never be forgotten. Not only is the beginning of the Christian life in the free and unconditioned grace of God but the believing Christian continues to live and work by the same grace. He is, as Luther puts it, *simul iustus et peccator,* sinner and saint at the same time. He never reaches in this life the point where he no longer needs divine forgiveness. "The man who is justified, just because he is justified, constantly returns to God with the cry: God be merciful to me, a sinner. The disciple must always pray: Forgive us our trespasses. And the church's prayer must always be: *Kyrie eleison!*" [8]

A believer is on a constant footing of war against the old sinful self-centeredness of human nature which not only finds it distasteful to live solely by what God gives but seeks to claim for its own the work of the Holy Spirit. "To the same extent that faith and its new life become our own possession, they become a part of our old man." [9] Failure to see that sanctification, like justification, is the gift of God, not our achievement, leads to the unevangelical idea that in sanctification the old man, now converted and in the process of being sanctified, proceeds toward sinlessness. The end result of such a process can be only the worst of all sins, spiritual pride, which may even be pride in one's humility.

[8] E. Stauffer, *op. cit.,* p. 292.
[9] Regin Prenter, *Spiritus Creator* (Philadelphia: Muhlenberg Press, 1953), p. 41.

A truly evangelical view of sanctification provides an escape from such a treadmill, for the grace of God sets us free from spiritual as well as carnal self-centeredness. When we acknowledge with Paul, "not I but the grace of God," the sanctifying Spirit is not diverted into the bottlenecks of our own spirituality but is free to flow through us to accomplish the tasks of love, a love that does not seek its own, not even its own sanctification.

To say that a justified believer is both a sinner and a saint does not mean that he is partly a sinner, partly a saint. In himself he is altogether a sinner, in Christ he is altogether a saint. Justification stresses the former aspect, sanctification the latter. Justification stands for the truth that without the grace of forgiveness man is nothing but a sinner, sanctification for the truth that "where there is forgiveness of sins, there is life." Koeberle, who in *The Quest for Holiness* has given a most thorough exposition of the relation between justification and sanctification, compares justification to a mother and sanctification to her daughter. The daughter cannot give birth to the mother, but she can destroy both herself and the mother. Our new life in holiness is born of divine grace, but our failure to make constructive use of it results in the loss of both holiness and grace. The merciless servant in whom the gift of forgiveness did not produce a forgiving spirit finds the forgiveness canceled. The exorcised demon returns to the house that remained empty, bringing with him seven demons worse than himself.

Justification and sanctification thus stand for two indispensable and inseparable aspects of living faith, justification for the intake, sanctification for the outflow, of divine grace. In justification faith receives the new life in Christ as a gift from the hand of God; in sanctification faith bears the fruit of the new life.

In the older post-Reformation theology sanctification is often described as "the new obedience," and obedience is indeed its primary characteristic. This is implied in the very word "Chriscian," Christ-man, belonging to him, under orders from him. In the life of our Lord there was one fundamental theme throughout —"Thy will be done." But he did not set up two standards, one for himself, another for his people. He expects of those who are his own the same obedience to God's will. Quite simply he says, "Follow me." Stewardship is nothing but a wholehearted response to that word. Its constant aim is to translate Christian thought and Christian speech into Christian action. Its watchword is "Not every one who says to me, 'Lord, Lord,' shall enter the kingdom of heaven, but he who does the will of my Father who is in heaven." [10] It therefore defines a Christian, not as one who believes what Christ taught, or even as one who believes in Christ, but as one who follows Christ in the obedience of faith.

This "practice of the Christian religion," as Dr. Greever pointed out, is the essential meaning of stewardship. And just as the doctrine of justification by faith lifts the curtain on the whole drama of redemption, so the doctrine of the priesthood of all believers summarizes the life of consecrated obedience. Spener, the seventeenth-century theologian who was among the first to see the doctrine in this light, also grasped clearly its implications for stewardship. "All Christians without distinction," he said, are "spiritual priests" who offer as sacrifice to God not only their prayers and their obedience to the Word but also their bodies, their hearts and tongues, their material possessions, their mind and will, their faithfulness in daily work, in a word, "*themselves,* with all that belongs to them, so that they desire no more to serve themselves, but only him who has purchased and redeemed them." [11] Stewardship, thus conceived, is nothing less than the distinctively Christian orientation to life as a whole. It concerns not only congregational or religious activity in the narrow sense but all aspects of the believer's life, both individual and social.

[10] Matt. 7:21.
[11] *On the Spiritual Priesthood of Believers,* questions 10-19.

Let us first make a few applications of the stewardship principle to individual life situations. Do I have the right to do as I please with my body and my physical health? If my body belongs to me, why not? If I burden my heart, strain my nerves, let my blood pressure rise, it is my own affair. But if I have given my body as a living sacrifice to God, if it is the temple and workshop of his Spirit, then it is a sin for me to impair or defile it.

The same is true of mental capacities. Have I the right to use my intelligence only to gain fame and comfort for myself? If my mind is independent of God, why not? But as a Christian I must take every thought captive to the obedience of Christ. I must love God with my whole mind and soul. So it is also with time. Time is God's servant and it is wrong to abuse it. It is the opportunity to work as God's partner. It must therefore be "redeemed," as Paul tells us. It must be freed from bondage to foreign powers and dedicated to the service of God. The same basic life attitude governs also the use of money and material property.

Money represents a person's own time, effort, brains, competence. It has been aptly described as personality in portable form. Yet the sins of covetousness and stinginess are usually forgotten sins, and many a man who regards himself as a Christian is actually their slave. If God has no partnership in a man's earnings, if he is not permitted to determine the use of a man's pocketbook, he has no real hold on the man himself. But if a man seeks *first* the kingdom of God and his righteousness, then the cause of the kingdom also ranks *first* in his use of money. How faithfully the early Christians translated this principle into actual practice is evident from the following passage in the *Didache*, the Teaching of the Twelve Apostles, which portrays the faith and life of the martyr church of the second century: "Every first-fruit, therefore, of the wine-press and the threshing-floor and of oxen and sheep thou shalt take and give to the prophets, for they are your high-priests. But if you have no prophet, give to the poor. If thou make a baking, take the first-fruit and give according to the commandment. In like manner, on opening a jar of wine or oil, take the first-fruit and give to the prophets; and of money, and raiment, and of every possession take the first-fruit, as may seem right to thee, and give according to the commandment." [12]

The social implications of the doctrine of the priesthood of all believers are uniquely important. To be a priest is not only to be consecrated but to be consecrated to serve. Thus in our Lord's teaching the total consecration of life to God, "You shall love the Lord your God with all your heart, and with all your soul, and with all your strength, and with all your mind" is inseparably connected with "You shall love your neighbor." To illustrate the operation of this genuine consecration, in contrast to a formal and compartmentalized priestliness, Jesus proceeded at once to tell the story of the good Samaritan. The exercise of true holiness can never be confined to the isolated privacy of individual lives, for love, its motivating power, is always directed toward others. And just as the kingdom of God is God's rule over all of life, so the stewardship of the kingdom can draw no artificial distinctions between individual and social, or sacred and secular. Kingdom people are the "salt of the earth" exercising a wholesome influence to check rottenness and to promote righteousness in all their earthly contacts. They are the "light of the world," radiant centers and transmitters of the true light that has come into the world. They are the "good seed" through whom the life of God is planted into the field of humanity.

The priestly function which Christians are called to exercise in social relations is closely related to the concept of "calling" which we studied in connection with the doctrine of creation. When the priesthood of believers is seen in its full context as based on the all-embracing character of the kingdom, motivated

[12] Translation by J. Fitzgerald (New York: Alden, 1884), section XIII.

by love, and realized in a total stewardship of life which gives sacred worth to the tasks of everyday living, it furnishes the key to a uniquely Christian social philosophy. Since I have presented the theological basis of such an approach elsewhere,[13] a few concrete applications must here suffice to illustrate this.

Basic among the orders of society is the family. The manifold problems which attend marriage and the home in modern society are being attacked from various points of view, the biological, the psychological, the sociological, the economic, the moral. But for a Christian solution to these problems the primary approach must be the theological. A psychologist, for example, can go no farther than to trace marriage to sex, a natural force like the hunger drive. From this point of view one form of sex satisfaction can have no intrinsic superiority over another. A sociologist, proceeding from a similar naturalistic starting point, can only regard monogamy as one form of sex adjustment among others, widely adopted and stabilized in the course of the centuries but likely to be supplanted by other forms as the mores change. But a Christian theologian sees monogamous marriage as founded upon the will of the Creator: "male and female created he them." Against the idolatry of sex he must point out that not even as a sexual being dare man play the role of God. We are not lords but stewards to whom the forces of life and fertility have been given in trust to use according to the purpose of the Creator. And the Creator has established the lifelong union of one man and one woman as the form in which they are to live their lives together.

Sex is not a mere biological tension to be released at random but the basis of a life partnership in love and loyalty. No amount of statistics concerning the violation of this norm can render it invalid, for it is grounded in the very nature of life, the structure of creation. And just as God meant men and women to be faith-

[13] *Resurgence of the Gospel,* chap. IV.

ful husbands and wives, he also meant them to be loving and responsible parents. Consecration to the will of God makes the home a divinely appointed place for the training of wholesome Christian personality. Christian fathers and mothers are priests and priestesses whose functions can never be performed by anyone else.

In the field of education a stewardship guided by the principle of universal priesthood has similar vital applications. Here too the starting point is the will of God the Creator as revealed in the Christ through whom and for whom all things were made. Thus the realms of science and art disclose their ultimate meaning in the light of God's purpose in Christ. Education ceases to be a conglomerate heap of odds and ends as it becomes integrated around this purpose and as consecrated stewardship furnishes the spirit and the atmosphere for all its phases and levels. Such education does more than supply information and develop various necessary masteries and skills. It provides an understanding of the goals to be sought and the spiritual controls needed to guide knowledge toward these goals. It prepares men and women to discharge intelligently the social responsibilities which they have in the service of God and fellow-men. Recognition of the fact that every useful occupation is a God-given calling serves both to stress adequate preparation for one's station in life and to prevent any artificial divorce between sacred and secular learning. The spiritual priests needed to carry out this concept of education are Christian teachers who not only command respect because of their professional competence but exert vital influence because they daily live out these educational ideals before their students. To cite a single example, thousands of men and women who studied philosophy at the University of Minnesota under David F. Swenson have carried with them an inspiring memory of such priesthood in action.

In the economic and political orders the conflict between the

Christian and the anti-Christian ways of life reaches its greatest intensity. The world of business and industry, representing a fierce struggle for survival and success and largely dominated by the false god mammon, tends to become a heartless jungle in which a genuine Christian love of neighbor is out of place. And the political state with its lust for power and its reliance upon physical force can become so demonized that "the prince of this world" can say, "It has been delivered to me, and I give it to whom I will." [14] It is in these areas, then, that the practice of Christian stewardship is most difficult. It is of course the task of the church to make the righteous will of God known not merely in general but also in its specific economic and political applications.

But the pronouncements of the church are likely to recoil harmlessly from the armor of embattled self-interest. It is through the priesthood of all believers, through Christian men and women acting as Christians wherever God has placed them, that the gospel can gain direct access into the strongholds of these principalities and powers. Putting to new use Luther's idea of "God's masks," we may think of Christians as the means by which God enters in disguise into places where the church as an institution cannot enter. What the church says about applying the will of God to the relations between management and labor may make but little impact upon the actual situation. The power of Christ is released much more effectively into these relations if the industrial executives and the labor leaders are Christian men who formulate their policies and make their decisions in the spirit of Christian stewardship.

The church has likewise the unquestionable duty to speak the truth to political power, but the most effective means for translating that truth into action are Christian citizens who bring into the exercise of their citizenship a lofty conception of

[14] Luke 4:6.

civic duty as God-given duty. No force is stronger than alert Christian conscience in checking the demonization of the state. Vigorous exercise of stewardship in the political realm is particularly necessary when human rights and human freedom are endangered, for it is only as free and responsible persons that men can be men in the Christian sense. Christians are committed to an unremitting struggle against any political order which denies the dignity and worth of individual persons, implied in the conception of a royal priesthood, or destroys the conditions under which Christian love can be practiced.

The priesthood of all believers supplies not only a Christian philosophy of life but also the necessary manpower for carrying out the mission of the church. In the early church it was, historically speaking, the force which enabled Christianity to get a foothold in the ancient world, to spread, and to triumph over the fiercest kind of opposition. "They went forth and preached everywhere, while the Lord worked with them." [15] This is a description of all Christians, not only of the apostles. Historians are generally agreed that primitive Christianity was primarily a lay movement. Its chief instrument of propagation was the witness, through life and word, of the rank and file of Christians.

With the passing of the age of martyrs and the growth of the church in worldly success and prestige, the royal priesthood of all believers was gradually transformed into an ecclesiastical theocracy. Priesthood became identified with a professional religious order mediating between God and ordinary Christians. Laymen were relegated to a more and more passive role, amounting in many cases to little more than nominal membership in a hierarchical organization which deprived ordinary Christians of any active participation in its work. In rediscovering the gospel the Reformation also restored the gospel's own vital method for releasing its power into the common life of humanity. Universal

[15] Mark 16:20.

spiritual priesthood was to Luther the fundamental working principle of the entire evangelical outlook. It enabled him to see the essence of the church in the apostolic communion of saints, the fellowship of Christ's people, not in a sacerdotal institution or any form of external organization. It led him to view the Christian ministry not as a mediatorial order but as a representative office through which the gospel entrusted to the entire fellowship comes into rightly ordered exercise. It caused him to abolish special sacred zones and to find true saintliness in the discharge of Christian responsibility within the natural orders of life in which God has placed us. One's everyday calling is above all the divinely given opportunity for witness, a summons to every Christian to be a unique outlet for the transforming power of the kingdom.

These dynamic insights of the evangelical heritage, which have once more been allowed to go into an eclipse, must be recaptured in the present day if stewardship is to serve its central purpose. In such a world as ours, in which large sections of the population even in "Christian" countries have become alienated from Christ and in which the Christian faith itself is challenged, the apostolate of the laity is an absolute prerequisite for the fulfilment of the church's mission. Chief credit for the mobilization of the lay forces of the church in America in our day must be given to the stewardship movement. By promoting "every-member visits" to bring into use all the resources of a congregation, by encouraging lay evangelism, by stimulating organized men's work, and by educating laymen to understand and to participate in the work of the church at large beyond the limits of the local congregation, this movement has pioneeered in liberating for the service of the kingdom the latent power heretofore frozen to the pews. This power must now be fully recognized and utilized not only on congregational, synodical, and denominational levels, but also on the ecumenical level. But if the church is to be the church, the royal priesthood of Christ's people, the world-wide witnessing and evangelizing messianic community, all its members must have a clear understanding of the truth of the gospel, be guided by positive Christian convictions, and be consecrated to the higher calling of the spiritual priesthood, whatever one's station in life may be.

In the final analysis, the doctrine of the priesthood of all believers is the answer to the central question of stewardship: what does it mean to be a Christian? The answer which the apostolic church gave to this question is summed up in a passage of Scripture which is one of the basic texts for the doctrine, Revelation 1:5-6, "To him who loves us and has freed us from our sins by his blood and made us a kingdom, priests to his God and Father, to him be glory and dominion for ever and ever."

This is a threefold answer. First, a Christian is one to whom Christ has given a genuinely fresh start in life. I was a slave and a prisoner, the apostolic writer tells us, but I was set free by the sovereign act of emancipation which took place on the cross. "Wretched man that I am! Who will deliver me?" This is our question of questions. This is the anxiety at the root of existence, which Kierkegaard portrays as "sickness unto death." Only Christ has the answer: "If the Son makes you free, you will be free indeed." He wipes the slate clean. He removes the guilt and breaks the power of sin. His sovereign gift of forgiveness of sins is the beginning and the constant pivot of the Christian life. This priceless treasure which men need more than anything else and which they can obtain nowhere else we have when we have Christ and his gospel.

Second, a Christian is one to whom Christ has given new resources for living. I was not only a slave, the apostolic writer tells us, but also a pauper and an outcast. "He made us a kingdom," or as a variant text has it, "he made us to be kings." He not only lifted me to the status of a free man but also filled my life with royal riches enabling me to live on the new high level.

Otherwise a freed slave falls back into slavery, a released prisoner drifts back into a life of crime. Not so with the newness of life in Christ. Our Lord compares the transforming power of the kingdom to a poor man's discovery of a treasure chest. He opens up new vistas of the divine potentialities of life, he awakens kingly thoughts in peasant hearts, he causes men to dream of kingdoms and thrones, and he makes those dreams come true. As Luther puts it, Christians are people who can say, "We are the Lords both in the nominative and in the genitive." Both with and without the apostrophe. Ours is the lordly life because we belong to the Lord. He puts an end to the meaninglessness and futility of our existence and endows us with the integrity and worth which God meant human lives to have. And he puts an end to our isolation from God and fellow-man by making us into a kingdom, giving us a life in fellowship in the beloved community which is God's plan for the corporate life of man.

Third, a Christian is one to whom Christ has given a new life purpose. My life, the apostolic writer tells us, revolved around my own petty self. Christ made me a priest. He took me off my own hands and gave me a new life in consecrated service. He gave me a new perspective, a new attitude, a new objective. He gave me new eyes with which to see in every man I meet a brother for whom Christ died and whom I must help to realize his share in the inheritance of the saints. A Christian, as Luther points out, never lives in himself. He lives in Christ through faith and in his neighbor through love. A Christian is one who has come to know the love of God in Christ and whose life has become a stewardship of that love.

And so with the apostles and the martyrs and the fellowship of the redeemed through the ages we say: To him who loves us and gave us this victory over sin, these resources of the kingdom, and this glorious priestly stewardship, to him, and him alone, be glory and dominion for ever and ever.

CHAPTER VIII

The Steward's Reward

"We have left everything and followed you. What then shall we have?" Peter, speaking for the twelve, asks this intensely human question in the sequel to the story of the rich young ruler.[1] Unlike the young man whose attachment to his great possessions had caused him to go away sorrowful, the disciples had gladly and wholeheartedly committed themselves to the stewardship of the kingdom. What then is the steward's reward?

In reply the Lord first directs the attention of the disciples away from the expectation of an immediate earthly recompense and places the thought of reward in the context of the final consummation of the kingdom. "Truly, I say to you, in the new world, when the Son of man shall sit on his glorious throne, you who have followed me will also sit on twelve thrones, judging the twelve tribes of Israel."[2] A steward of the kingdom, a partner of the Messiah, is not "like a hireling who looks for his wages."[3] His eye is upon the glorious fulfilment of the divine purpose in which he is privileged to share. The point of this phase of the reply may be illustrated by the replies of three men engaged in a building project to the question of what they were doing. One said, "I am laying bricks." Another said, "I am making twenty dollars a day." But the third replied, "I am building a church."

After providing an insight into the ultimate goal, a vision of the new world, the Lord goes on to relate the satisfactions of the eternal kingdom to present existence: "Every one who has

[1] Matt. 19:27-30. Cf. Mark 10:28-31; Luke 18:28-30.
[2] Matt. 19:28.
[3] Job 7:2.

left houses or brothers or sisters or father or mother or children or lands, for my name's sake, will receive a hundredfold." [4] Mark adds to this description two significant phrases: "now in this time" and "with persecutions." The joys of the kingdom are experienced here and now, not merely in some distant future. But they do not provide a carefree earthly utopia but strength with which to face the hardships of a hostile world. To emphasize the unique character of the reward as a sovereign gift of God, which does not depend on men's own efforts, both Matthew and Mark conclude with the Lord's words, "But many that are first will be last, and the last first." Matthew then proceeds to record the parable of the laborers in the vineyard, in which every trace of merit disappears altogether, and everything, the reward as well as the opportunity to work, is a matter of divine grace.

In the light of this teaching it is obvious that the gospel gives the concept of reward a new meaning quite different from its ordinary connotation of compensation or remuneration for services rendered. Alexander Cruden expressed the evangelical meaning of reward well in the quaintly beautiful language of two centuries ago: "that free and unmerited recompense which shall be given to the godly by the goodness, bounty, and mercy of God, after all their labours in his service. This is a reward wholly of grace, in respect of us, or our deserving, but of justice on account of the purchase of it by the sacred treasure of Christ's blood, and the unchangeable tenor of the gospel, wherein God promises heaven to all obedient and true believers." [5] This definition contains the distinctive twofold emphasis which we have already discovered in our Lord's teaching and which we must now examine more closely, namely, the sovereignty of grace and the perspective of eternity.

[4] Matt. 19:29.
[5] A. Cruden, *Concordance*, note on "Reward."

THE SOVEREIGNTY OF GRACE

The thought of reward based on merit is diametrically opposed to the gospel. The latter is the good news that God out of sheer love offers the blessings of his kingdom to all men as a gift without any regard to human achievement. The disciples' question, "We have left everything. . . . What then shall we have?" shows that they had not yet grasped the essential meaning of the gospel. Such a question belongs in the legalism of the Old Testament but has no place in the New. In asking it Peter shared the prevailing Jewish view which Bishop Gulin has summarized as follows: "In giving his chosen nation the law God set this nation in a privileged position among the nations of the world. Thereafter an Israelite had to demonstrate with his life that he was worthy of the trust which God had placed in him. By works in keeping with the law he had to accumulate with God a treasure on the basis of which God would justify him at the last judgment. Through obedience to the law a man achieved merits for himself, and God would one day reward him for these." [6]

There are sayings of Jesus which seem to fall into this pattern of thought. "The measure you give will be the measure you get." [7] A man who gives alms, prays, or fasts "in secret" will be openly rewarded by the "Father who sees in secret." [8] A man who does good to the poor who cannot repay him "will be repaid at the resurrection of the just." [9] Those who suffer for righteousness' sake are assured: "Your reward is great in heaven." [10] Seen in their context, however, such sayings do not repudiate the gospel but only prepare the way for a true appreciation of it. Most of them occur in the Sermon on the Mount, where Jesus presents a righteousness totally transcending that of rabbinic legalism and presupposing the free resources of the messianic kingdom. Never does Jesus present the kingdom in terms of

[6] E. G. Gulin, *Uuden Testamentin Teologia*, Helsinki, 1940, pp. 156-57.
[7] Matt. 7:2.   [8] Matt. 6:4, 6, 18.   [9] Luke 14:14.   [10] Matt. 5:12.

wages which a man earns by keeping God's commandments. A good steward does his duty because it is his duty, not for the sake of the reward. "Does he thank the servant because he did what was commanded? So you also, when you have done all that is commanded you, say, 'We are unworthy servants; we have only done what was our duty.'" [11] A reward there is indeed for the good steward, but it represents not wages or merit but "the goodness, bounty, and mercy of God." True stewards can accept it only with humble and grateful amazement: when did we perform these acts of divine worth which are accredited to us? [12] The reward comes as a surprise because it had played no part in the doing of the work. The heart had been so completely in command that not only had the left hand been unaware of what the right hand was doing but the head had not been asked to make calculations or keep records. The works had been the works of overflowing love, and the reward is the reward of immeasurable grace.

The new content which our Lord gives to the concept of reward as an expression of God's sovereign grace appears most clearly in the story of the laborers in the vineyard. [13] Here the point of view of law and merit is specifically contrasted with the point of view of grace. The contrast is represented by two groups of workers, the grumbling and the trustful, the ones with a hireling's attitude and the ones with a child's attitude. The former appear to have reason for complaining, for they have borne the burden and the scorching heat of a twelve-hour day and yet receive only the same compensation as those who have worked only a single hour in the cool of the late afternoon. Yet the legality of the employer's action is beyond question, for the workers get exactly what they had bargained for. But those who complain that they are not getting enough receive a meager reward indeed, even though all the legal demands are fully met. For in this vineyard everything—the call, the work, the reward—is sheer grace.

Hence those who commit themselves to the stewardship of the kingdom, who give themselves to the Lord's service without watching the clock or counting the cost, receive a richer reward than they ever expected. The man who deals with God on the basis of merit receives only what he deserves and that is not much. The man who works not for the reward but for the Lord discovers that the Lord not only keeps his promise but gives far more than he promised. In the kingdom every day is payday, for communion with God is the supreme blessing, and sharing in his life and work is its own reward. If the service itself is a privilege and not a drudgery, then the longer and fuller it is, all the greater is the intrinsic reward. A poet whose name I do not know has expressed this beautifully:

"Lord of the Vineyard, whose dear word declares,
Our one hour's labor as the day's shall be;
What coin divine can make our wage as theirs
Who had the morning joy of work for Thee?"

No one has grasped this supplanting of the point of view of merit with that of grace more clearly than the apostle Paul. The gospel which he preached was a constant repudiation of the belief that man's proper relation to God is based on the law and supported by man's conformity to it. It is based on the promise of free salvation fulfilled in Christ and it is supported by divine grace alone. Paul draws a sharp contrast between "one who works," receiving his reward in the form of "wages that are his due" and "one who does not work" but trusts in the divine promise and receives his reward as a gift.[14] Contrary to all considerations of justice, God shows his sovereign grace when he "justifies the ungodly." This same grace determines the content of the reward expected by the steward of the gospel. "What then is

[14] Rom. 4:4-5.

117

my reward?" asks the apostle, and replies, "Just this: that in my preaching I may make the gospel free of charge, not making full use of my right in the gospel." [15] He is referring to the principle, "Those who proclaim the gospel should get their living by the gospel," which he has just eloquently defended. But the steward-ship of the gospel of grace is such a glorious privilege in itself that he pushes all ideas of reward aside as entirely secondary. His thought follows the same line as that of George Herbert Palmer, who upon being called to teach at Harvard found such joy in his work that he exclaimed, "And to think that I was even paid for it!" To a distributor of the riches of God's grace both the work and its reward, like the message he proclaims, are sheer unde-served privilege.

THE PERSPECTIVE OF ETERNITY

In the light of the gospel our thinking about reward is directed not only from merit to grace but also from earth to heaven. When earth rewards the steward only with suffering, he is told, "Rejoice in that day, and leap for joy, for behold, your reward is great in heaven." [16] It is the long look of eternity that clarifies the ultimate issues of stewardship. The gospel teaches us both to place stewardship in the perspective of eternity and to place eternity in the perspective of stewardship. Both of these lessons may be learned from our Lord's profound words, "Truly, truly, I say to you, he who hears my word and believes him who sent me, has eternal life; he does not come into judgment, but has passed from death to life. Truly, truly, I say to you, the hour is coming, and now is, when the dead will hear the voice of the Son of God . . . for the hour is coming when all who are in the tombs will hear his voice and come forth, those who have done good, to the resurrection of life, and those who have done evil, to the resurrection of judgment." [17]

First of all, we cannot appreciate the true meaning and worth

[15] I Cor. 9:18.　　[16] Luke 6:23.　　[17] John 5:24-29.

of Christian stewardship unless we see it in the perspective of eternity. One who hears my voice, says our Lord, and commits himself to me in faith "has eternal life." The gospel on which our stewardship is based brings eternal life into the lives of men here and now. Eternal life is never a matter of the mere future. It is not a "beautiful isle of somewhere," a distant land somewhere at the end of the trail. It is a new dimension which the living Christ gives to the life which his people are living now. *Aionios,* the New Testament word for "eternal," refers to the new aeon which Christ brought into the present age. Christ's people already share in the life of the new aeon. They live in expectation of the day when the King will say to them, "Come, O blessed of my Father, inherit the kingdom prepared for you," but they are already sons of the kingdom. They wait for the day when death will be swallowed up in victory, but the Easter triumph already gives them access to resurrection power with which to wage a victorious struggle against the forces of evil. They look for the return of their Lord in glory, but he is already a living reality in their midst. They cannot express their hope of heaven in any higher form than as the perfection of the communion they already have with him.

The application of the perspective of eternity to the present life is made most clearly in the Gospel of John. The believer does not merely wait for eternal life but has it. He will not come into judgment, for he has already passed from death into life. The Lord who is the resurrection and the life gives his own the solemn assurance: "Whoever lives and believes in me shall never die;" "truly, truly, I say to you, if any one keeps my word, he will never see death." [18] But the same thought appears also in other New Testament writings. According to Paul, believers already "share in the inheritance of the saints in light" for "he has delivered us from the dominion of darkness and transferred

[18] John 11:26; 8:52.

us to the kingdom of his beloved Son." [19] And the author of Hebrews declares that while "we do not yet see everything in subjection to him," already "we see Jesus . . . crowned with glory and honor . . . bringing many sons to glory . . . the pioneer of their salvation." [20] It is passages of this type that give support to the various forms of modern theology which refuse to restrict eternity to a realm at the end of history and seek to interpret afresh its meaning for present historical existence. To the historian von Ranke every point of time was equidistant from eternity. To Harnack Christianity meant eternal life within the stream of time. In the "axiological" aspect of his eschatology Althaus sees every wave of time washing the shore of eternity. Dodd's "realized eschatology" insists that in the historical mission of Jesus the kingdom has already come and references to a future coming are only symbolic. Bultmann's demythologized existentialism transfers the Christian hope from a future event to a present decision to accept eternal life from the hand of God. In the main body of Barth's theology the future consummation of the kingdom is pushed aside by the thought of a transtemporal realm surrounding us now but tangible only through Christ. Hence it is always appropriate to say, "The Lord is at hand."

Exclusive preoccupation with this line of thought carries the danger of disregarding what the Word teaches on eternal life in its future aspect. The gospel presents the kingdom of God both as a present experience and as the complete fulfilment of the divine purpose in the future. Without forgetting the latter, however, we do well to view our present stewardship of the kingdom under the aspect of eternity. We are thus enabled to see things from God's point of view, to distinguish between the transient and the permanent, and to relate what we are doing to the plan which God is realizing in history. We are children of time, and without the perspective of eternity we see life only

[19] Col. 1:12-13.   [20] Heb. 2:8-10.

as a succession of passing events. In scriptural language this is time as *chronos*, as mere duration, time which, "like an ever-rolling stream, bears all its sons away." But there is another kind of time, God's time, expressed by the word *kairos*. It cannot be measured by clocks or calendars but by the fulfilment of God's purpose. We have an inkling of such a higher standard of measurement when in our own experience we may pack into a few unforgettable hours more living than has been contained in many uneventful years. Just so in the midst of the rolling centuries there are *kairoi*, moments full of divine significance. They give meaning to the rest of history because they mark the realization of God's plan for the world. Thus our Lord began his ministry with the proclamation, "The *kairos* is fulfilled, and the kingdom of God is at hand." [21] And Paul uses the word in describing the plan according to which God has determined for the nations their allotted times and fixed a day on which he will judge the world.[22] The *kairoi*, taken together, constitute a history of redemption, which furnishes the key for a Christian interpretation of history as a whole. They reveal the penetration of the temporal by the eternal, the working of God's mighty arm as he directs the events of time toward their ultimate goal.

The specific bearing of the concept of *kairos* on stewardship is pointed out by the apostle Paul in Ephesians 1:9-10, the profoundest of all stewardship texts, one in which the thought of stewardship is gloriously transfigured by the light of eternity. God, declares the apostle, "has made known to us in all wisdom and insight the mystery of his will, according to his purpose which he set forth in Christ." This purpose he defines as a "stewardship plan," *oikonomia*, for "the fulness of the *kairoi*" to integrate all things in heaven and on earth into a Christ-centered whole.

[21] Mark 1:15.   [22] Acts 17:26, 31.

121

Here the concept of stewardship is applied to God's eternal plan of salvation revealed in the *kairoi* of history, with Christ himself as the supreme steward. But the apostle also makes clear in the context that Christian believers, those who are "in Christ," have been "chosen from the foundation of the world" to share in the divine stewardship plan. In a similar passage Paul uses his own ministry of the gospel as an example of a Christian's participation in God's plan to save the world: "I became a minister according to the divine *oikonomia* . . . to make fully known, the mystery hidden for ages and generations but now made manifest to his saints. . . . For this I toil, striving with all the energy which he mightily inspires within me." [23] It is because his activity is geared to the fulfilment of the divine purpose, not to the passing show of the world, that for the believer time becomes transformed from *chronos* into *kairos*. Time becomes charged with eternity when it is an opportunity to labor in the service of the eternal gospel.

Thus Paul encourages both the Ephesian and the Colossian Christians, to whom he has presented this sublime conception of stewardship in the perspective of eternity, to "make the most of time," [24] to actualize its character as *kairos*. But this privilege of rising above the limits of temporality to share in what God himself is doing brings heaven to earth. In Paul's language, believers blessed with such spiritual blessing already move "in the heavenly places." [25] This is the intrinsic reward which the Christian steward already enjoys.

We have seen that the steward's reward appears in its true light when we place stewardship in the perspective of eternity. The gospel also teaches us to place eternity in the perspective of stewardship. We may speak with Kierkegaard about a "double movement of eternity," not only of the movement of eternity toward us but also of our movement toward eternity. Like Paul,

[23] Col. 1:25-29.　[24] Eph. 5:16; Col. 4:5.　[25] Eph. 1:3.

we are led by contemplation of the rewarding nature of the gospel to envisage the steward's ultimate reward, the incorruptible crown which is waiting at the finish of the earthly race. This is also the sequence of our Lord's thought in the fifth chapter of the Gospel of John. After affirming that the believer already has eternal life and will not come into condemnation, he proceeds to speak of the final judgment and resurrection. The Son of God, he declares, has not only the power to give eternal life now through his Word, but he has also the authority to determine ultimate destiny. "The hour is coming when all who are in the tombs will hear his voice and come forth, those who have done good, to the resurrection of life, and those who have done evil, to the resurrection of judgment." [26]

This is the distinctive Christian approach to life after death. How different it is from other approaches has not always been clearly understood. Confronted with the tragic fact of death, the human heart has sought various ways to get around it. Poets have sensitized their imagination to "the touch of the vanished hand and the sound of the voice that is still." Philosophers have speculated on the invincible surmise of possible survival. Plato, the greatest of them, wonders whether the soul might have an existence of its own which the death of the body cannot disrupt, and whether a soul which identifies itself with imperishable values might not itself take on imperishability. Aristotle is content to believe that while nothing can prevent the disintegration of personality, there is in man a detachable element, reason, which lives on. The mystical philosophy of India offers the thought that after a long series of repeated incarnations man may finally win release from the wheel of existence and lose his identity in the ultimately real as a dewdrop loses itself in the ocean. In modern Western thought the hope of immortality rests principally upon the alleged intrinsic and indestructible worth of personality,

[26] John 5:28-29.

which emboldens a man to say with Goethe, "Why should a coffin impose on me?"

Common to all these speculations is the idea of an inherent and unbroken continuity between this life and the next. They question the factual reality of death and assume that man has within himself the power to leap over the grave into another existence. The fanciful nature of this hypothesis has led scientific thinkers to say that the hope of immortality rests on wishful thinking. Desiring to keep on living and refusing to part from their loved ones, so say the psychologists, men try to escape reality by building imaginative bridges into another world. The truth in this charge is enough to demolish most non-Christian arguments for immortality and to invalidate many an Easter sermon based on such arguments. But it has no bearing whatever on the gospel of Jesus Christ.

The Christian doctrine of life after death is the exact opposite of wishful thinking. It teaches not some kind of fanciful continuity but the fact of death and the fact of resurrection from the dead. Both facts are based on God's righteous governance, not on man's desire. Whether we desire to abolish physical death, or become annihilated, or survive, the facts remain unaltered.

God has decreed that "the wages of sin is death" and that "all who are in the tombs will come forth." The ground for our belief in life beyond the grave is not man's power to defy death but God's power to raise man from death. And the content of this belief is not continuity but responsibility. Particularly significant is the twofold character of the resurrection, "Those who have done good, to the resurrection of life, and those who have done evil, to the resurrection of judgment." The stewardship emphasis on man's personal accountability to God thus reveals its ultimate importance. Our destiny is not determined by our wishes or surmises but by the righteousness and mercy of God. Eternal death is his judgment on sin and from that judgment

124

there is no appeal. Eternal life is the gift of his grace to those who have responded to it in faith. To the believer whose account with God is squared by the grace of justification, whose hope is built on nothing less than Jesus' blood and righteousness, who knows that there is no condemnation for those who are in Christ Jesus, this is glorious gospel. But it gives no comfort to one who is not in Christ. It deprives him even of the rest he has sought in the grave. Even there he must hear the voice of God summoning him to give an account of his life. Death can deliver no one from the reach of God. It only opens the door to the hall of judgment. "We must all appear before the judgment seat of Christ, so that each one may receive good or evil, according to what he has done in the body." [27] But those who know the Judge as Savior know the perfect love that casts out fear and have confidence on the day of judgment.

Thus the same gospel which provides stewardship with the perspective of eternity also places eternity in the perspective of stewardship. The truths which we have discovered to be the fundamentals of stewardship, the righteous omnipotence and the saving grace of God, the lordship of Christ, the high responsibility of those who are privileged to share in the fulfilment of God's own purpose, the abiding worth of works performed out of grateful and self-forgetting love, the unfathomable depth of the joy which attends faithfulness in the Lord's service, these are finalities which remain when heaven and earth have passed away. But whether we think of the close of our own workday when one by one we receive the summons, "Give an account of thy stewardship," or lift our eyes to the consummation of God's plan for all of life in the triumphant return of Christ to judge the living and the dead, the vision of the ultimate goal should give incentive to a more vigilant and faithful performance of the work now entrusted to us. This is the emphasis which runs

[27] II Cor. 5:10.

through all of our Lord's teaching on stewardship. "It is like a man going on a journey, when he leaves home and puts his servants in charge, each with his work, and commands the door-keeper to be on the watch. Watch, therefore, for you do not know when the master of the house will come, in the evening, or at midnight, or at cockcrow, or in the morning—lest he come suddenly and find you asleep."[28]

There are many things about the future that we do not know. But we do know that the future belongs to Christ. And we know that what he expects of his stewards is above all faithfulness. And we know that new and more glorious opportunities to serve him will be entrusted to us in the higher stewardship that awaits us when we hear his voice, "Well done, good and faithful servant; you have been faithful over a little, I will set you over much, enter into the joy of your master."[29]

[28] Mark 13:34-36.   [29] Matt. 25:21.

Type used in this book
Body, 10 on 13 and 9 on 11 Janson
Display, Garamond
Paper: Standard White Antique RRR